Shattered *also gives hope to the betrayer—that beyond error often lies redemption. The spiritual nature of humankind is given center stage to extend direction to those violated and those who perpetrate.*

Dr. J. Kent Griffiths, Doctor of Social Work,
Licensed Clinical Social Worker,
Licensed Marriage and Family Therapist

The issue and feelings of betrayal are so huge that people are often overwhelmed in their ability to approach it, more or less work through it. In this step-by-step guide, the authors have generously thought through the necessary steps and given the wounded person a blueprint for healing. At a time when minds are scrambled and functioning is low, a blueprint to the path of recovery is a good tool to have. So often, tools are too complicated for a time when the wounded's energy is tied up in grieving and sorting out their future. Keeping the steps simple and the tasks well spelled out, the wounded is coached through the maze of healing with partners (the authors) on each side of them.

This book is good for those who desire to work through their issues on their own and also a good tool for therapists who want an approach to use in counseling that is not overwhelming to the wounded. Like tools for a builder, this tool belt for recovery is loaded down with available resources and ideas for working one's way through the heartache of betrayal.

Sandra L. Brown, MA, Psychotherapist and
Author of *How to Spot a Dangerous Man
Before You Get Involved*

Pornography has become an "invisible affair" for millions of individuals whose partners do not consent to this form of infidelity in their relationship. Despite those who claim pornography is harmless fun, many lives are devastated by its impact. Shattered *offers insight and perspectives for those wanting to confront and overcome this form of emotional and physical betrayal in relationships.*

Rory C. Reid, Licensed Therapist, and Co-Author of
Discussing Pornography With a Spouse: Confronting and Disclosing Secret Behaviors

This book is filled with clear explanations and concrete examples of the devastating phenomenon of betrayal, which continues to wreak havoc in increasing numbers of lives and families. Fay Klingler and Bettyanne Bruin offer specific suggestions and sound encouragement for recovery, along with the knowledgeable insight of people who have been there. More than anything else, this book is a beacon of hope.

Carolyn Campbell, Author of
Reunited: True Stories of Long-Lost Siblings Who Find Each Other Again

Betrayal and loss of trust can have many faces in a variety of relationship situations and often end up leaving the betrayed party with feelings of loss, guilt, anger, depression, and absolute emptiness in trying to face each day. Klingler and Bruin give hope to those who have lived in the pain and darkness of betrayal (no matter what the cause), and gently guide them on their journey into the light, as they take their lives (and their power) back. Real people's stories combined with a focus on unending faith provide love, kindness, and hope to all who seek to heal.

Mary Jo Fay, R.N., M.S.N., Speaker, Columnist,
"Survivor," and Author of *Get Out of Your Boxx
and Live the Life You Really Want!*

PRAISE FOR SHATTERED: SIX STEPS FROM BETRAYAL TO RECOVERY

We define healthy self-esteem as "the experience of being capable of meeting life's challenges and worthy of happiness"—and being responsible and accountable for our actions and results. This vibrant book meets our definition throughout. Shattered *is a "proactive book." It makes you think as you read. And if you apply just one of the ideas, you'll be well on your way to recovery and forgiveness.*

Sharon Fountain, President, National Association
for Self-Esteem; http://www.healthyselfesteem.org

While the adult entertainment industry basks in its 60-billion-dollar-a-year profits from the production and distribution of explicit materials, marriages are being devastated by the impact of pornography at an unprecedented rate. Readers of Shattered *will find straightforward answers to confronting all forms of infidelity and sound counsel on recovering from these forms of emotional betrayal, including the impact of pornography on committed relationships.*

Bishop George Niederauer , Catholic Diocese of
Salt Lake City and President,
Utah Coalition Against Pornography

Shattered *offers a powerful look into the lives of individuals who have suffered the devastating effects of betrayal and worked through the process of recovery. There is no shortage of information and advice offered to victims of abuse. However,* Shattered *picks up where other books leave off. This book breaks the recovery process into six manageable steps that focus on all aspects of recovery from physical to emotional and beyond, realizing that all elements must be addressed to truly recover from the effects of betrayal. This book focuses on the fact that recovery is a process that can have wonderful, lifelong, and positive changes for good.*

Rebekah Clements, Zero Tolerance to Domestic Violence Program Coordinator, Weber County, Utah

Shattered *is a most beneficial tool in the recovery of a betrayed person. It chronicles in a clear, systematic way on how to navigate the different phases of betrayal. The Domestic Violence movement realizes that there are many stages on this journey from victim to survivor and each stage is plagued by adversity.* Shattered *is a wonderful guide to keep at hand to let you know that what you are feeling is quite common, and most assuredly, that you are not alone. I also believe that what* Shattered *has to offer is applicable to any difficult situation, not just betrayal. I know that I will recommend this book to any woman making the transition from victim to survivor. I truly think it's fabulous!*

Barbara J. Wandyes, Executive Director, the R.O.S.E. (Regaining One's Self-Esteem) Fund, http://www.rosefund.org

I have been waiting for a book like this since I began my counseling career in 1974! Shattered *sets aside theory about what causes betrayal and moves to concrete application of problem-solving skills in dealing with the losses of betrayal.*

The theme of this vibrant book is that blaming and rage rob one's soul of energy and peace. Promoted is the power of healing and of moving forward after hurt. The reader is guided to personal growth, accountability, and even forgiveness—yet is taught clearly about setting boundaries to unacceptable behaviors.

Shattered

Six Steps From Betrayal to Recovery

Fay A. Klingler
and
Bettyanne Bruin

Mapletree Publishing Company
Denver, Colorado

Printed in the United States of America
09 08 07 06 05 1 2 3 4 5 6

Cover design by Tamara Dever www.tlcgraphics.com

Library of Congress Cataloging-in-Publication Data
Klingler, Fay A.
  Shattered : six steps from betrayal to recovery / by Fay
A. Klingler and Bettyanne Bruin.
  p. cm.
  ISBN 0-9728071-9-5 (alk. paper)
  1. Betrayal. I. Bruin, Bettyanne, 1955- II. Title.
        BJ1500.B47K58 2005
        158.2—dc22
                        2005006805

Printed on acid-free paper

Mapletree Publishing Company
Denver, Colorado 80130
800-537-0414
e-mail: mail@mapletreepublishing.com
www.mapletreepublishing.com

The Mapletree logo is a trademark of Mapletree
Publishing Company

We dedicate this book to those who have suffered betrayal and yearn to not just survive but thrive. Our hearts, sympathies, and well-wishes go out to you.

Shattered is the fragile egg, betrayed.
Left battered, shocked, confused, and dismayed.
Like Humpty after his great fall,
Scattered in pieces at the base of the wall.
Assaulted, deceived, bereaved in pain,
Can Humpty ever be put together again?

Table of Contents

Chapter One, Awareness 1
Ask to see things as they really are. Trust your instinct. Acknowledge reality. Look for the signs.

Chapter Two, Acceptance 17
Acknowledge and accept your reality and take responsibility for your future. Emotionally disconnect. Recognize patterns of behavior. Manage your fear and anger.

Chapter Three, Action 37
Get on your knees and ask for God's blessings and direction, then stand on your feet and do what is right. Act, don't just react. Consider what you want from the confrontation. Consider where you will confront. Consider when you will confront. Consider how you will confront. Observe quietly. Set reasonable limits. Consider how you will evaluate the confrontation. Try again. Ensure your safety. Take the risk of making life better. Rely on God. Trust what you know to be true.

Chapter Four, Authorization 83

Give yourself permission to talk, to listen, to rebuild trust, and to act with confidence. Share your experience with family. Share your experience with friends. Write your experience in a journal. Look to others for support. Develop faith in God. Trust and care for yourself. Seek professional help when necessary. Rebuild your trust in mankind.

Chapter Five, Accountability 113

In fairness, hold yourself and others accountable, and free yourself through forgiveness so you can visualize beyond your past and look with hope into the possibilities of the future. Own your part in the betrayal. Develop your bill of rights. Hold others accountable. Forgive the other person. Forgive yourself.

Chapter Six, Advancement 139

With belief in yourself, take charge of your life, and chart a new course to advance and bloom. Visualize your camp. Control the outcome. Follow a plan. Commit time and effort. Create balance. Believe in yourself. Lighten your load. Serve others. Keep your perspective.

Foreword

by Thelma Soares
Mother of Lori Hacking,
whose life ended because of betrayal

This book is a significant breakthrough—it should be the required reading "handbook" for everyone who has ever been betrayed. Fay and Bettyanne have gone to great lengths to bring awareness to the physical and emotional abuse of betrayal that temporarily clouds the minds and destroys the hearts of many innocent people. The title, *Shattered*, describes exactly how I feel, and as I read the book, I am impressed with the timeliness of its message and Fay and Bettyanne's insight borne of personal experience. I wish I'd had this book years ago as I was struggling through a painful divorce.

Domestic violence is still considered to be primarily physical abuse, and while great efforts have been made to reduce the degrading and disgusting behavior of physical abuse, emotional abuse—specifically in the form of betrayal—has yet to be fully recognized for its tragic and devastating effects. Unlike physical abuse, emotional abuse leaves no visible physical scars but instead penetrates unseen to the very core, leaving in its wake silent, debilitating destruction of the inner spirit. What follows betrayal is a lengthy struggle (usually many years) to understand and deal with this emotional and mental trauma.

My daughter, Lori Hacking, suffered the ultimate betrayal, and her death has changed my life and the lives of my extended family forever. I do not now, nor I may ever in this life, comprehend everything that went so wrong amidst a world that seemed so right. I will mourn for her until the day I die. The domino effect is in full force. But the wisdom found in *Shattered* and the loving support of people around the world have helped me cope with this tragedy.

I hope Lori will be remembered for the remarkable young woman she was and for her natural ability to find the best in everyone she met. My heart goes out to all those who find themselves, through the goodness of their hearts, in a situation similar to hers. May you have the courage and fortitude to take the necessary steps now to protect yourself against being innocently caught up in a web of lies or tolerating anyone who attempts to break you down through any type of physical or emotional abuse—specifically in the form of betrayal.

May those who have suffered from the effects of betrayal find the peace and solace you need to move beyond this highly misunderstood and painful act to the life you desire and deserve.

Lori was an exceptional student at the University of Utah, where she received the President's Award for outstanding scholastic achievement. She was selected as the George S. Eccles Intern in Business Policy through the Hinckley Institute of Politics. She was also nominated for membership in Beta Gamma Sigma, the honor society for collegiate schools of business. Lori graduated cum laude in December 1999 with a bachelor's degree in Management. In her honor, the Lori Kay Soares Hacking Memorial Scholarship is awarded to a woman in the David Eccles School of Business who is disadvantaged through abuse, family difficulties, or other life circumstances, providing tuition for her junior and senior years. Contributions to the scholarship fund can be made online at rememberlori.com or lori.utah.edu, by calling 1-800-561-LORI, or by mailing contributions to: Lori Kay Soares Hacking Memorial Scholarship Fund University of Utah Development Office, 201 Presidents Circle, Room 302, Salt Lake City, UT 84112

Everyone is invited to honor Lori's memory by making a contribution to her scholarship fund that will share the values and ideals she exemplified with future generations of students.

Thelma Soares

Foreword

by *Rita Smith*
Executive Director, National Coalition
Against Domestic Violence

Devastating emotional violence is what a person feels after being victimized by one who has betrayed.

The authors of *Shattered* have put together an empowering book, including firsthand accounts of what it feels like to be innocently absorbed into, survive, and escape the painful world of betrayal. There are no miracle cures for abuse and violence. The advice and counsel provided in these pages can provide a path away from the violence. It comes from those who have been there, experts who know all the ins and outs of this life-altering tragedy and how to recover and once again lead a happy, successful, and productive life.

Betrayers may think they are not doing anything wrong. Or they may think they won't get caught, or that they can talk their way out of any given situation. If they can't talk their way out of it, they may think the consequences will be too light to necessitate a change in their behavior. But in reality, the betrayer or abuser is solely responsible for choosing his or her actions.

The suggested steps in *Shattered* enable a betrayed person to break the vicious patterns of victimization. These steps are based on an individual's core beliefs and his or her ability to build healthy self-respect and self-value; to act, not just react; to develop strategies for creating and achieving sound goals and overcoming obstacles.

There are many local domestic violence programs that provide batterer's education or intervention services in communities across the United States. If you would like to talk to someone or find out about the domestic violence resources in your community, contact the National Domestic Violence Hotline, 1-800-799-7233, or go to www.ndvh.org.

Rita Smith

Acknowledgments

I used to think my story was unique, but I've learned that's not so. On the one hand I find it sad because that means, like me, others have been deeply hurt. But on the other hand, I find it exhilarating because it shows we share a resiliency, a desire to make life good in spite of our traumatic experiences.

I've enjoyed working with Bettyanne on this project. Through this effort, we have grown more confident and learned skills from each other. My awesome husband, Larry, has been patient and immensely supportive. He is my companion and my best friend, whose charity, gentleness, and integrity warms my heart from day to day. My wonderful parents, Miles and June Alldredge, remain two of my anchors. Their examples of hard work and integrity have kept me afloat. My children, step-children, and grandchildren continue to teach me and make my life happily full.

To my family and supportive friends, I shout a resounding cheer of thanks to you all!

Fay A. Klingler

First and foremost, I would like to acknowledge my parents: My mother, who taught me how to love, and my father who taught me how to survive every obstacle life, at times, presents. Without these two traits, life's problems would have defeated me long ago.

I would like to acknowledge my seven children, who somehow have known, through every one of life's tragedies, how to face them with this same, natural love and strength.

My children have truly given me enough love and hope, through their care, concern, and independence, to last a lifetime. I would also like to acknowledge all of the many friends who have picked me up, over and over again, including my brothers, sisters, in-laws, and ex-in-laws, for the kindness they have shown me through the years. And to my husband, Kent, together we have truly made *climbing uphill* an interesting and fun experience. Thank you, so much, for all of your incredible determination and resiliency.

Bettyanne Bruin

Whether a book is long or short, there are many people responsible for its creation and production. *Shattered* is no exception. We are deeply grateful to all who contributed their thoughts, stories, and experiences, enriching the text of the book. Without their willingness to divulge their private lives, *Shattered* would not have been written. We are also thankful to Dr. Richard L. Williams for reviewing and contributing to the work, and to Pam Moody, who spent valuable time reading and commenting on our first draft. We extend to Thelma Soares our appreciation for her support and contribution to this book as well as to the cause of physical and emotional abuse awareness. We also express our thanks to the National Coalition Against Domestic Violence for their ongoing dedication, support, and energy in the fight against abuse. And we offer a large thank you to our publisher, editors, and all who helped produce the finished product, making it possible for us to share our message of recovery.

Introduction

You have been betrayed. Perhaps at this moment, you cannot imagine how your life could be put back together. What does the future hold for you? How do you get this type of traumatic pain behind you? Can you ever trust again?

The pain of betrayal is excruciating. This particular kind of victimization is emotionally all-encompassing. Yet, unlike Humpty Dumpty, you can, with the help of a strong, external support system and a firm, internal belief system, put your life together again.

Betrayal is defined as the act of not being loyal to a person who believes you are loyal to him or her, often by doing something that hurts that person. Synonymous words showing up in the thesaurus are: cheating, dishonesty, duplicity, treachery, disloyalty, deception, and perfidy. One definition of perfidy sums up well the act of betrayal: A deliberate breach of faith; a calculated violation of trust.

Be it an affair or leading a double life, the consuming pain created in the wake of betrayal is nearly insurmountable. Gone is trust. Erased is the reality of what one's life was expected to be. True love is replaced with feelings of being used. Reasoning of the human mind can scarcely take in all of what happens with this subtle crime. Betrayal is often unseen, has no smell, no sound, no whistling bells or honking horns. But it creeps, little by little, into a person's life, and for hours, days, years, or a lifetime a person can be victimized without even realizing it, until the betrayal is identified.

Having suffered the devastating effects of betrayal, or perfidy, as described above, Fay Klingler and Bettyanne Bruin, at one time, perhaps like you, wondered how they would ever put their lives back together. Yet, with the help of family, friends, professionals in the field of betrayal, great books, faith and prayer, years of hard work, and forging ahead (sometimes, it seemed, against all odds) they survived, and *you can too.*

During their survival process, Fay and Bettyanne, individually, met many people who also survived betrayal. These betrayed but courageous people shared their stories about survival and how they have since built emotionally healthy lives. As a result of meeting these incredible people, a collaborative book emerged.

Shattered is meant to help and encourage all who desire to recover from this unwelcome, uninvited devastation, whether you are the one who was betrayed, the loved one of a betrayed person, or someone who hopes to avoid ever being betrayed.

Interwoven within this carefully scripted book are the stories of exceptional people who found a way to recover from one of life's biggest traumas. Their stories are real, but other than Enid Greene (whose story is nationally known), their identities have been masked to prevent any violation of confidence. In sharing their true-life accounts, Emily, Martha, Sarah, Todd, Enid, Whitney, Kami, and Barbara illustrate the emotional bombs that were unexpectedly dropped onto their hearts and temporarily shattered the well-being of their lives. There are remarkable similarities in their sources of strength to recover. This is the magic of it all—the power of the human mind and heart that allows a person to overcome all odds and re-emerge emotionally healthy.

Emily was an editor taken advantage of by her writer friend Ann.

Martha struggled with her husband over finances.

Sarah found porn sites on the history of her husband's computer.

Todd's wife left him for another man.

Enid's husband duped her, embezzling her campaign funds and "borrowing" millions of dollars from her father.

Whitney chose to stay in her marriage, even after discovering her husband was having an affair.

Kami feared her violent husband would take her life.

Barbara experienced the pain of her husband's repeated indiscretions.

As these individuals and various aspects of their stories are discussed, you may want to refer to the index in the back of the book, where they are listed by first name, in order for you to be able to follow their stories.

All of the factors for your recovery are encompassed in *Shattered*. You just need to recognize and act upon these survival skills. In this book, professionals in the field of betrayal recovery show how to enjoy all the happiness life, love, and laughter can bring. Fay and Bettyanne would now like to join whatever motivation caused you to pick up this book and help you move forward to regain the life you desire and deserve.

We begin with the story of Emily....

CHAPTER ONE

The First Step—Awareness

Real knowledge is to know the extent of one's ignorance.—Confucius

Little did Emily realize when she met Ann at a writers' conference that her world was about to be turned upside down. And understandably so. Ann was an older, intriguing person with an international background.

A professional editor, Emily felt uncomfortable when Ann was with her, but still she pursued the relationship. Her instinct or gut told her Ann would use her, but her brain said she could learn from her. Ann appeared knowledgeable about women from other countries, and Emily wanted to gain some of that knowledge.

Ann was in the process of writing a book. As an editor and as a new friend, Emily offered to look over her materials. Ann was an exceptional writer, and Emily learned a lot by reading Ann's work.

The more work Emily did for her, however, the more Ann requested. She would call at Emily's office to tell her she just faxed over another piece of her book. "Could you take a look at it *now?*" Ann asked. "I need it for a meeting with my publisher this afternoon."

1

Emily's daughter said Ann was using her because she only called when she wanted something. Emily's husband began to resent the time she gave to Ann. At last, the pressure became so great that Emily felt she had to confront Ann.

The next time Ann called, Emily told her she couldn't work any longer for free. Ann said, "Oh, you didn't think I was going to let you do all that work for nothing, did you? Of course I'm going to pay you. The next time I see you, I'll give you $500. I really need you to take a few minutes, though, and look at the piece I just faxed to you. Could you do that?"

Of course the money was never paid. And without explanation, the phone calls and requests ceased for several months. Then out of the blue one day, Ann called and said sweetly. "Hello, Emily, did you think I had dropped off the face of the earth? You could have called me, you know!"

Emily's gut said, *This is manipulation. She's trying to make me feel like I failed to do something so I'll feel obligated to say yes to what she is going to ask.* And sure enough, another request was made.

Who was the betrayer and who was the betrayed?

Emily admits she allowed the *using* to go further than she should have. "I just gave her too much benefit of a doubt and didn't speak up from the start about what I would and wouldn't take. I did learn from her, but I should have asked to be paid in the beginning."

Trust Your Instinct

Martha's husband was always unpredictable and moody. Sometimes he was physically abusive to her and to the children. But she wanted so badly for the marriage to work that she bandaged reality, bandaged it with so many layers the wounds were hardly visible.

Because she could not tolerate contention, she never stood up to him for any length of time. "I used to think of myself as a mouse, actually," she confides. "I just couldn't stand arguing or the ugly feelings that followed. I admit I was afraid of him. I knew if I pressured him for information about finances, he'd threaten to hit me. So I learned to let it go for long stretches of time."

Martha admits her instinct hinted something was wrong, something way beyond his loss of temper.

"One day, I was walking with a neighbor and she told me how she heard of men having private post office boxes to hide mail from their wives," said Martha. "I told my neighbor my husband would never do anything like that!" She remembers briefly weighing the possibility in her mind, but honestly believing what she said about him.

A week or so later, Martha was looking for something in her husband's nightstand drawer and noticed an envelope addressed to him. But the address wasn't for the home—it was for a post office box. When she first confronted him, he made light of it and turned the conversation around, asking why she was prying through his things. When she pressed the confrontation further, he got angry. "Loud and angry," she remembers. Taking a risk, she stood her ground and insisted the post office box be closed and demanded there be no more secrets. She requested to know everything about their finances and asked to take over the bill paying. Their explosive conversation died down with his agreement.

Even after what he claimed to be full disclosure, Martha's uneasiness increased. The months that followed were filled with tension and lots of questions. "Now tell me again why we have this bill," she pleaded with him. His answers were elusive and accompanied with anger. "I was exhausted," Martha said. "Trying to persist with the pulling and tugging for information wore me out. So I fell back into my old, mousy pattern and gave the finances back to him. He promised to pay off the loans and get us out of debt."

As the years passed, Martha's uneasiness grew. "Sometimes I'd look at him and wonder if he was leading a double life. I even commented to him once, 'It feels like we're in two different worlds, like there's a whole part of your life I don't know about.'" But she never pressured him beyond the surface. "I should have followed up on that gnawing feeling," she said later.

The marriage lasted nine more years. That uneasy feeling was so strong by then that Martha did something she'd never before had the courage to do. "I knelt in prayer," she said. "I asked God, 'Let me see things as they really are.'" She pleaded over and over to see reality.

Reality hit like suddenly opened floodgates. Her teenage son suspected his father had stolen his savings from his bank account and asked Martha to investigate. The bank confirmed her husband had removed $200 each month, leaving nothing in her son's account. Her husband claimed the bank made a mistake.

Her ecclesiastical leader called to ask Martha if she knew about all the welfare money that had been provided by the church to her family over the past months. He didn't seem surprised that she was totally unaware. By investigating, she found the money had been used to pay for their motorhome and boat, along with her husband's business long distance calls.

She found over forty charge cards and loans with her name attached. When she called the banks and companies, the answers to her questions were always the same. "But I don't know anything about this loan," she would say. "How did my name get on that card? I didn't apply for it." The response: "We have your signature on the application."

4

Collection agencies started calling. Loans that her husband told her had been closed were still owing, with increased balances. And yes, there was again a secret post office box!

Who was the betrayer and who was betrayed?

Acknowledge Reality

Although they were innocent betrayers, in the sense that they allowed or enabled Martha's husband and Ann to take advantage of them, Martha and Emily betrayed themselves. Often during her marriage, Martha felt uneasy. Like Emily, she admits she was partly to blame. "I should have followed up on that gnawing feeling."

Fundamentally, Emily and Ann did a trade—editing for knowledge. A trade, that is, until Ann said she was going to pay but never did. There was no real harm done, other than a loss of time and money for Emily perhaps. But in Martha's case, that enabling held an expensive price tag, a life-changing domino or ripple effect that made a difference for her and for everyone who knew her.

Whether consciously or unconsciously, Martha chose to deny or ignore reality. But what is denial? As defined in *Webster's Dictionary,* denial is "a refusal to acknowledge." In this case, Martha refused to acknowledge her instincts and the warnings and happenings of real life. In fact, what she really did was create a *reality* that worked for her but was far from *real.*

According to Dorann C. Mitchell, a licensed clinical social worker with a diploma in psychoanalytic psychotherapy, "Denial is an unconscious defense mechanism that must be called into the conscious mind before decisions can be made regarding a person's reality." (Dorann C. Mitchell, in interview with Bettyanne Bruin.)

With this thought in mind, it is important to understand that *healthy denial* is an instinctive self-defense or coping mechanism that helps a person adjust to traumatic situations, like death or divorce. This type of denial is a temporary, slowly releasing state of shock that can soften the blow of troubling events. However, *unhealthy denial* is the tool that stops an individual from seeing (and effectively dealing with) another person's harmful words and actions. In the case of unhealthy denial, the other person's harmful words retreat into the betrayed's subconscious mind. The result is a masking of the facts and an unwillingness to recognize and respond to reality.

When reality is out of control or difficult to manage, a person may attempt (either consciously or unconsciously) to stay in his or her comfort zone and not deal with the pain. Instead, he or she might retreat into the safe cave of denial, where a person can be surrounded by the feeling that everything is under control.

Because of the manipulative tactics used by the betrayer, denial is sometimes difficult to understand and identify. Some forms of denial include:

■ Ignoring or allowing any kind of abusive behavior
■ Overlooking the obvious or just skimming across the surface of a problem
■ Disregarding or burying one's instincts
■ Letting important things pass by
■ Creating a delusional world that helps one to cope

Dorann C. Mitchell also states, "Some might feel that denial is a wonderful place for a person to be, but it certainly creates a lot of problems for the people around him or her as they scramble to fill in the blanks for the person unable to deal with real life" (ibid.). In this case, the person unable to deal with real life is the person being betrayed.

In addition to disregarding her instincts or that "gnawing feeling," as she put it, Martha's fears got in the way of her accepting reality. "I couldn't fail! It never even entered my mind that I could allow our marriage to end. But looking back, I see I went overboard in my attempt to make it succeed. I think he took advantage of my unquestioning, complete commitment." Martha continues, "There were many times I feared him. At one point in our marriage, I realized it wasn't safe to leave the children with him. He was so unpredictably explosive. So I tried not to go out in the evenings, once he came home." In the name of commitment, Martha continued in the relationship. "I had to make it work," she stated.

When a person is in the state of unhealthy denial, the world of reality threatens to disrupt how the person wants life to be, which is one of the reasons why a person backs off so easily and continues to ignore things as they really are.

Martha often bypassed the *who, what, where, when,* and *why* of volatile issues. She told herself she needed to think the best of her husband and make the best of the situation (which is one of the traits of a person prone to denial). Until she asked to see things as they really were, Martha followed the victim's creed that "people don't lie, especially to the one they love." She skimmed over important details, and, blinded by her commitment, moved on, never even questioning her husband's integrity.

By the time Martha ceased to deny reality, her husband had crossed so many lines that, to her, no more lines could be drawn. With nothing more to lose, reality replaced her fear of loss. The more she investigated, the more she found. Finances were not the only problem. Before their divorce was final, Martha discovered her husband had secretly married another woman in another state.

Denial's greatest ally is fear—fear of what one might lose. As long as a person fears losing something, denial has a place to grow.

Change can only happen in the *real* world.

Look for the Signs

Sarah was a confident, outgoing mother of four. But, when month after month she consistently found porn sites on the history of her husband's computer, she feared the worst. Was Richard hooked on pornography? Had he stepped out on her? And if he had stepped out on her, should she leave him? How would her children survive without a father? Afraid of what answers might come as a result of those questions, fear became Sarah's driving force. Once again, as she had done so many times in the past, Sarah set the issue aside, denying its importance.

As mentioned before, not all denial is bad. A healthy dose of denial can be a blessing at a time when a situation in its entirety is too painful to accept. With the death of a loved one, for example, it is fortunate that denial sets in and allows a person to accept the unacceptable in small doses. But in Martha's situation and in Sarah's case, denial became an unhealthy tool used to avoid dealing with the problems that encompassed their painful realities.

In the case of betrayal, once the stage of denial is passed, reality must be explored. Who is the betrayer? Why does one person betray another? How does a person know if he or she has been betrayed, and what are the signs to look for?

8

Unlike Emily and Martha, true betrayers do not act from a point of innocence. They have a hidden, selfish agenda. They want something and intend to get it regardless of any moral cost. Deceptive and disloyal, they are ready to betray a trust to fulfill their goals. Their faithlessness can lead to seduction, emotional or physical abuse, or desertion.

Betrayers do not discriminate. Men and women are both betrayed. Victims include the wealthy and the poor, the young and the old, the educated and the uneducated.

Why do they betray? For some, it is as simple as wanting something for nothing, like Ann befriending Emily to get editing without paying for it. For others, it is because they have developed that pattern of living— either by watching someone betray another to achieve a goal, or by practicing betrayal themselves, little by little deceiving others and getting away with it. As a person becomes accustomed to deceit, lying feels more comfortable than telling the truth. Some individuals simply find reaching their goals easier through betrayal rather than through acts of integrity. Others enjoy the thrill of conniving and manipulating to fulfill a plan.

Betrayal comes in many forms. These forms can be termed as follows:

■ Emotional betrayal

At times hardly noticeable, emotional betrayal is the act of manipulating someone's mind to achieve a specific purpose. It may be gaining support by telling someone you love them, when in reality your affection is seated elsewhere. In other words, emotional betrayal includes leading an individual to believe one thing when you know reality is something else. It can be a withholding of information or communication. Or it could be ridiculing someone or directing his or her thoughts to produce the feeling that he or she is incapable of doing anything other than what the betrayer asks to be done.

■ Financial betrayal

Financial betrayal is using someone's name or money without consent, or refusing to spend money on things that are necessary. Financial betrayal can also be exerting power to control, such as in the case where a man ensures his wife has no financial independence or, on the other hand, where he exploits her earning ability.

■ Environmental betrayal

This type of betrayal is conducted through fear. Often it prevents the betrayed from ever breaking free. For example, the betrayer gains an individual's confidence and then exerts power over him or her, either physically or mentally, so the individual feels isolated and fears the negative consequences of talking to others or seeking help outside the betrayer's environment.

Environmental betrayal may also include neglect, such as not responding appropriately to illness or injury.

■ Sexual betrayal

Sexual betrayal may be adultery or just a flirtatious affair. It also includes inappropriate intimate demands, such as when a woman is ill or recovering from childbirth and her husband tells her he loves her, but insists he must have sex now, even though it may be harmful to her health.

Regardless of the term, betrayal occurs whenever someone, especially an individual perceived to be trustworthy, violates another. Betrayal is usually subtle, but almost always involves determined manipulation and deceit.

Like a whale rising to the surface for air, betrayal has its surface points. These points come up like dots in a dot-to-dot book. But it's not just the connecting dots, like unpaid bills or observations of porn on the Internet, that create a clearly drawn picture. What dwells in the spaces between the dots is just as important, and sometimes far more, than what becomes visible on the surface. Some signs or spaces between the dots might be:

■ Unreasonable defensiveness and a resistance to open communication or participation

Most questions, especially to an intimate partner, should not generate resistance. A defensive attitude can be a sign that the partner is protecting someone, something, or a certain situation.

Emotionally healthy people usually don't feel threatened by being asked to respond to questions. If an individual truly cares about another person and is anxiously concerned about their well-being, he or she will do whatever it reasonably takes to help him or her work through concerns or questions. When it comes to healthy relationships, if a reasonable question is asked in a reasonable manner, a reasonable answer should be expected.

■ Minimization/maximization

Minimizing can be compared to a telescope. The focus on you is enlarged while the focus on him or her is reduced. Many times, in the face of betrayal, minimizing/maximizing takes place, meaning one minimizes the problem while attempting to maximize the focus somewhere else. "If you think I have problems, what about the guy down the street? My problems are little compared to his." Your relationship, however, isn't with the guy down the street. So that kind of statement is not a valid comparison but an effort to distract.

Minimizing might also be reducing the act to a generalized judgment. "Your concerns are so petty." A concern is not petty when it comes to a wife having no idea where a husband has been, and then he comes home at two in the morning, smelling of women's perfume. What caring person minimizes his or her partner's feelings as petty?

■ Entitlement

Continually there are right choices and wrong choices placed before us. Within a couple's relationship, there are issues, standards, activities, and behaviors both parties agree to abide by within the framework of, and out of respect for, the relationship. These commitments or understandings become the *right* things to do. Actions and decisions made outside this agreement become the *wrong* things to do. Sometimes, as in the case of betrayal or other matters of discontent within marriage, entitlement enters the picture. When this happens, entitlement becomes just another word for rationalization.

Professionally, when time is invested in a job, a worker is entitled to receive a paycheck because performing his or her duties and receiving pay in return is the agreed *right* thing to do. An employee is entitled to be paid. However, entitlement is wrong when it is used to protect a *wrong* thing or choice—used to justify or rationalize. In this case, it becomes a warning sign or a waving, red flag, as in the case of a marriage where a certain couple agreed both partners would work to pay their bills. When the husband reneged on his end of the deal, the wife complicated the situation by the distraction of entitlement. "Because I work and not you," the wife said, "I am *entitled* to spend money any way I see fit, even if it means paying three hundred dollars of my hard-earned money for this pair of pants instead of paying the bills we agreed on."

Instead of reframing a *right* path for the couple by discussing why the partner couldn't work, or if he could, when and how, the wife chose actions based on what she felt was right for her personally, ignoring her responsibilities to the relationship.

Many times, a betrayer, in his or her mind, uses entitlement as a means of justifying behavior. Oftentimes, this unreasonable behavior surfaces in a betrayer's normal expression of thoughts, ideas, or explanations of actions or events.

■ Manipulation

"You're crazy, I wouldn't do something like that." "You're making it look worse than it really is."

Betrayers are usually good at playing mind games. They take advantage of your trust and your willingness to take what he or she says as truth and question only yourself. The betrayer's fabricated *truth* becomes your *reality*.

■ Rationalization

Rationalization comes in the form of excusing a partner's poor behavior. "Bill had to leave for three days. But it's okay that he didn't tell anyone where he was going because he's under so much stress at work."

Loving, intimate relationships do not work this way. A partner does not leave for three days without telling where he or she is going. An enabler makes excuses for his or her partner to create in the mind's eye a fantasy that represents the person they wish to be married to.

"My wife drinks because her father did." In reality the wife's father did not force her to drink. She drank because she chose to drink. Using rationalization to excuse poor behavior is enabling because, when it really gets down to it, there is *no* excuse for poor behavior.

Can you show up for work late and rationalize that you never learned as a child to be on time? In certain situations there is cause to understand and make room for human error. But rationalizing chronic behavior is simply a form of denying reality.

■ Guilt transference

One tool of the betrayer is shifting blame to someone else. "If only you wouldn't make me so mad, then I wouldn't have to lie." The person being betrayed plays into the betrayer's hand when he or she becomes convinced the greater problem or solution is with him or her, not with the betrayer. To deflect responsibility, instead of focusing on the lie, the betrayer concentrates his or her efforts on the person being betrayed. Convinced the betrayer is rational and reasonable, the person being betrayed tries to find ways to make personal changes that will positively affect the betrayer. "Maybe if I was a better listener (more patient, more open-minded...) like he says, then he wouldn't have to lie to me." "Maybe if I was nicer, then she would want to come home to me instead of that other guy."

An individual's choice to lie (or to commit adultery) is a character flaw that has nothing to do with anyone else's choices or behavior.

■ Emotional disconnection or consistent preoccupation—the "anybody home" syndrome— coupled with unexplained agitation and anger

Betrayers might stare off in the distance as though in another world, or shrug their shoulders and appear not to care about important issues. They may have a delayed reaction or no reaction at all to real-life situations, or never reveal their emotional thoughts or feelings. When emotional disconnection occurs, a person can become so preoccupied with his or her *hidden* thoughts that unexplained agitation takes place as the outside world becomes a nuisance to the disturbing thoughts inside. It is as though the person *checks out*— builds up a wall to protect his or her secrets or hidden motives.

■ Coercion

Coercion is the use of force, either real or implied, through fear and intimidation, especially in response to something that is not necessarily wrong. A betrayer might say, "If you call your mother like that again, I'll shut off our long distance." "Do what I say, or else there is going to be trouble." And most of these unreasonable attempts to coerce are to cover a world unknown to the person being betrayed.

Most attempts to coerce begin with the word *if* or include the words *or else*.

For the victim of betrayal, the desire to be loved and the desire to trust are far more powerful than the desire to see reality or to believe someone is betraying him or her. But like early cancer detection, if the shield of denial is lowered and the first signs of betrayal are discovered and confronted, there can be hope for repair, hope of a turn in the road—a healthier path followed, and a hope of healing.

The first step in recovering from betrayal is awareness—awareness of the role one plays both as the betrayer and the betrayed. Awareness leads an individual to accept reality. Acceptance of reality gives him or her the ability, power, and energy to take action and bring about change.

The first step–Awareness

Ask to see things as they really are.

I am aware of:

_____

_____

_____

_____

_____

_____

_____

_____

_____

_____

_____

_____

_____

_____

CHAPTER TWO

The Second Step—Acceptance

There can be no hope of changing something until we recognize and accept exactly what that thing is.—Author unknown

Discovering and accepting acts of betrayal are two different things. Some individuals lack the self-respect to believe they are worthy enough to stand up for themselves. Some fear abandonment or physical harm to themselves or their children. Even though they discover betrayal, they choose to rationalize or ignore it, or in some cases even enable it, in order to keep things at a status quo. They feel powerless to act, as though they have been put in a box with the lid locked tight. Some say they feel emotionally paralyzed.

Acceptance can only occur when an individual makes a conscious choice to gather the facts and face them with action. The betrayed must desire to know the truth—to live in reality—as mentioned in Chapter 1. Only then is the pain of betrayal felt, which is a vital part of the recovery process. What follows is a tidal wave of emotion, an overwhelming sadness, and a heavy feeling of loss. But it is only by working through this pain that an individual gains freedom and peace.

Acceptance means you, as the betrayed, are finally willing to take the risks necessary to stop the continuing betrayal. To accept something, you must come to know the facts for what they really are. In order to do this, you have to open your senses and interpret the signs written on the walls and ceiling of that sealed box you're in. What are you really dealing with?

Todd and Jan pushed the limits of their finances too far, and mutually decided she would go to work outside the home. During the ensuing two years, Jan met a man at work who became a close friend. "Over time, they would go to lunch together, and eventually, even company parties held on Sunday took priority over attending church with me and our son," said Todd. "During the summer, we flew to Atlanta to visit my family. Due to work, Jan could only stay for one week. My son and I stayed for another week or so. One evening, Jan called and spoke with both of us. She asked how everything was going. I said everything was great. We said our goodbyes. And then, after hanging up, I felt something was wrong. I couldn't put my finger on it, and pretty much disregarded it."

Frequently during the next year, Todd and his son went to church without Jan. She grew increasingly distant. Todd remarked, "She began sleeping in our guest room. Intimacy between us entirely disappeared. Her friend from work came to our home one evening when I was not there. They saw each other often.

"The writings were on the wall," Todd said, "the distancing from me after my return from Atlanta, the pains it seemed she bore as though something had been broken and could not be reassembled, and a self-esteem/ self-preservation mode that intensified over the weeks and months following my return.

"Often I was so pained from what was happening that I allowed my self-sorrow to surpass good judgment.

I would go into the guest room, now her room, to find letters she and her friend exchanged to identify the depth of their relationship. I don't remember the exact contents of those letters, but they only served to confirm my fears, and increase my anger toward her friend."

Finally, one day while Todd was at work, Jan's friend came and helped her move out to an apartment she had located elsewhere in town. Betrayal is marked by small indiscretions that usually lead to bigger ones.

Emotionally Disconnect

You, as the betrayed, must emotionally disconnect with the betrayer long enough to objectively look at your behavior and his or hers. This might sound harsh, but there's no other way to accurately see what is happening. You have to let go of controlling what you see. So often those who have been betrayed paint unrealistic pictures of themselves and what is happening in their lives in order to take away their pain.

Disconnect emotionally so you don't *fix it* in your mind, like Martha did. "I would say to myself, 'Maybe I'm wrong. Maybe it's just me. I must be exaggerating what he's doing. If I try harder, everything will be okay. Tomorrow will be different.'" And then she would paint over all the writing on the walls of her box so she couldn't see clearly, so it looked nice and felt nice once again, except for that *gnawing feeling*.

Ask questions. Consider asking other people, not necessarily the betrayer. Look outside the box. Remember how Martha went to the bank instead of to her husband to find out what happened to her son's savings? Gather the facts as unemotionally as possible. If it helps, write down what you find from different sources so you can cross-reference them.

Recognize Patterns of Behavior

Look for consistent patterns of behavior, behavior that intimidates or degrades you, behavior that harms or exerts control over you. Be observant of the little things that add up, like words the other person uses to manipulate how you feel about him or her, the situation, or yourself—"Why, you know I wouldn't have done anything like that if you hadn't..." Step back and watch for how the other individual excuses himself or herself from any wrongdoing or tells a truthful-sounding but still untruthful story.

Workers at the Lanark County Interval House, a shelter for abused women and their children, found that the women at the shelter expressed concern that the abuse they encountered wasn't serious enough to warrant a plea for help. The shelter workers gave them a list and a highlighter and asked them to mark incidents they experienced. They explained that many of the actions listed in isolation might be considered innocent. But in combination and over a period of time, they might constitute a pattern of behavior designed to break another person's spirit. By working through the list, many of the women were amazed to see the number of abusive actions they experienced.

The list the shelter workers used was originally compiled by an Ottawa men's group, New Directions. Many of its members had been convicted of assaulting their partners and were asked to list behaviors they used to control or harm their wives or girlfriends. The list doubled with further input from victims of abuse, workers in women's shelters, and members of the Lanark County Coalition Against Family Violence.

Try going over the list yourself and highlight any that apply to you. An asterisk (*) indicates actions that may be criminal, depending upon the circumstances.

Note that the list is written for women, but applies to men, and to children, in some situations, as well.

■ Using emotional abuse

♦ Making her do illegal things*
♦ Making false accusations
♦ Making verbal threats
♦ Yelling
♦ Intimidating
♦ Making her think she's crazy or stupid
♦ Overpowering her emotions
♦ Disbelieving her
♦ Bringing up old issues
♦ Inappropriately expressing jealousy
♦ Degrading her, finding fault, name calling
♦ Turning a situation against her
♦ Laughing in her face
♦ Withdrawing communication, silence
♦ Refusing to do things with or for her
♦ Insisting on always getting his own way
♦ Pressuring her
♦ Neglecting her
♦ Expecting her to conform to a role
♦ Expressing real or suggested involvement with other women
♦ Making her feel guilty
♦ Using degrading mannerisms, such as snapping fingers at her
♦ Threatening to get drunk or stoned unless...
♦ Starting arguments
♦ Withholding affection
♦ Punishing her by not sharing in household chores
♦ Holding grudges, never really forgiving
♦ Lying
♦ Treating her as a child

- Having a double standard for her
- Saying one thing, meaning another, brainwashing her, manipulating her
- Denying or taking away her responsibilities
- Failing to keep commitments
- Threatening her with the loss of immigration status
- Deliberately creating a mess for her to clean up
- Threatening to report her to the authorities
- Making her drop charges
- Telling jokes that belittle or indicate hatred toward women
- Refusing to deal with issues
- Minimizing her work or contribution
- Pressuring her to stay while drugs or alcohol are being abused
- Coming home drunk or stoned
- Withholding whereabouts, not coming home
- Having pictures that indicate hate or violence against women
- Egging her on, challenging her to engage in physical violence
- Friendshipping or supporting men who are abusive
- Demanding an accounting of her time and routine
- Taking advantage of her fear of something
- Putting her on a pedestal
- Ridiculing her food preferences
- Threatening or promoting suicide unless...
- Refusing to allow or forcing her to use contraception
- Forcing her to have an abortion
- Refusing sex on the grounds that her pregnant body is ugly
- Denying that the child is his
- Refusing to support her during the pregnancy

- Refusing to support her during the birth
- Denying her access to her newborn child
- Refusing to support her or help out after she comes home with the baby
- Blaming her because the infant is the *wrong* sex
- Refusing to allow her to breast-feed
- Sulking or making her feel bad for time spent with the baby
- Failing to pass on messages
- Putting down or ignoring her in public, making a *scene* in public
- Denying her access to family or friends
- Interfering with her family or friends, being rude to her friends or relatives
- Changing personality with others
- Dictating her mode of dress
- Dictating her behavior
- Habitually choosing friends, activities, or work rather than being with her
- Censoring her mail
- Treating her like a servant
- Not giving her space or privacy, insisting on accompanying her into the doctor's office
- Assaulting her in front of the children*
- Initiating false child abuse charges against her
- Making her stay at home with the children
- Teaching children to abuse their mother through name-calling or hitting
- Embarrassing her in front of the children
- Taking no responsibility for the children
- Threatening to abduct the children or telling her she'll never get custody
- Threatening to kill or injure the children unless…
- Putting down her parenting ability
- Buying the children's affection with expensive gifts

- Failing to show up on time to pick up children or not having them back on time
- Pumping children for information about their mother's boyfriends
- Telling children their mother is responsible for breaking up the family
- Using children to transport messages
- Denying her access to the children
- Failing to supply a valid phone number
- Forcing her to participate in or witness rituals

■ **Using financial abuse**

- Taking her money*
- Forging her name*
- Giving her false receipts
- Canceling her insurance
- Sabotaging her efforts to attain economic freedom
- Withholding money
- Spending money foolishly or beyond means
- Pressuring her to take full responsibility for finances
- Failing to pay fair share of bills
- Failing to spend money on special occasions
- Spending on addictions, gambling, sexual services
- Pressuring or controlling her working conditions, preventing her from taking a job
- Keeping family finances a secret

■ **Using environmental abuse**

- Harming pets*
- Ripping clothing*
- Locking her in or out*
- Throwing or destroying her possessions*
- Slamming doors, punching walls
- Throwing objects or food

- Denying her use of the phone
- Mowing over her garden
- Driving too fast*
- Driving recklessly, pounding the steering wheel*
- Driving while intoxicated*
- Forcing her into a vehicle*
- Pushing her out of a vehicle when it's in motion*
- Threatening to kill her by driving into an oncoming car*
- Chasing or hitting her with a vehicle*
- Injuring her in a deliberate accident*
- Hitting her while she's driving, grabbing the steering wheel while she's driving*
- Prohibiting her from using a vehicle by tampering with the engine, taking the keys
- Putting his foot over hers on the gas pedal
- Controlling what she does, whom she sees and talks to, what she reads, and where she goes, making her account for herself

■ Using sexual abuse

- Forcing unwanted sexual contact, hounding her to have sex, uttering threats to obtain sex*
- Forcing her to have sex with others*
- Forcing her to have sex with animals*
- Pinching, slapping, grabbing, or poking her breasts or genitals*
- Forcing sex when she's sick or after childbirth or surgery*
- Knowingly transmitting sexual diseases
- Treating her as a sex object
- Pressuring her to pose for pornographic photos
- Displaying pornography that makes her feel uncomfortable
- Using sex as the basis or solution for an argument

◆ Criticizing her sexual ability
◆ Forcing unwanted fondling in public
◆ Expecting sex while purposely not washing
◆ Calling her names, such as whore, slut, frigid, bitch
◆ Accusing her falsely of affairs
◆ Degrading her body parts
◆ Telling sexual jokes or making sexual comments in public
◆ Demanding sex for drugs or alcohol
◆ Demanding sex as payment or trade
◆ Administering drugs or alcohol for sexual advantage
◆ Insisting on checking her body for sexual contact

■ Using physical abuse
◆ Forcing any unwanted physical contact*
◆ Kicking, punching, pinching, pulling, pushing, slapping, hitting, biting, or shaking her*
◆ Cutting or burning her*
◆ Butting her head, pulling her hair*
◆ Squeezing her hand or twisting her arm*
◆ Choking or smothering her*
◆ Force-feeding her*
◆ Spitting on her*
◆ Throwing her or throwing things at her*
◆ Hitting her with objects or whipping her*
◆ Restraining her in any way*
◆ Urinating on her*
◆ Breaking her bones*
◆ Knifing or shooting her*
◆ Threatening to kill or injure her*
◆ Ignoring her illness or injury, hiding or withholding necessary medication
◆ Denying or restricting her food or drink
◆ Pressuring or tricking her into alcohol or drug use

■ Using religious abuse

- ◆ Using religion to justify abuse or dominance
- ◆ Using church position to pressure for sex or favors
- ◆ Using her then demanding forgiveness
- ◆ Spending excessively for religion
- ◆ Interpreting religion his way
- ◆ Preventing her from attending church
- ◆ Requiring sex acts or drug use as religious acts
- ◆ Mocking her beliefs

(Fern Martin and Dr. Catherine Younger-Lewis, "More than meets the eye: Recognizing and responding to spousal abuse" *Canadian Medical Association Journal,* Dec. 1997; Vol. 157, pp. 1555–1558, used by permission of the publisher.)

Do you see a correlation with your highlighted items and that *gnawing feeling* you have? Do you see a destructive pattern of behavior in your spouse or in yourself?

Sometimes in the process of investigating and uncovering the facts, the betrayed begins to identify how he or she may have contributed to the betrayal. Guilt is a byproduct of this discovery—guilt because the individual let it happen, or guilt for that part the individual didn't see coming and thinks he or she should have. These reactions are normal, but must be dealt with in a realistic manner.

If the relationship is repairable, both parties have to let down their guard and their pride and take action to mend the wounds. If the betrayal is so severe that a remedy cannot be found, many feelings, including overwhelming sadness, will be the result. Accepting the loss of an intimate relationship is a process similar to grieving over a loved one's death. Life is never the same.

If a person is dependent upon the betrayer, self-preservation may be the reason the betrayal is ignored.

Survival instincts may be the cause of the temporary blindness. Try to be honest with yourself. Trust that *gnawing feeling.* Look unemotionally at what has happened. Allow your self-respect and integrity to shine by how you view the facts. How do they fit with your personal value system? Do you understand that what you've been told is not what happened? Do you see a breach of trust?

Ask yourself, "What kind of person am I dealing with?" Role-play as though you were a neighbor to someone experiencing the items you highlighted on the list. How would you view and react to these situations?

As you gain information and come to terms with your reality, *what happened and how* may come clearly to light and flood you with feelings of fear and anger. The *why,* on the other hand, may be far more elusive. Often the *why* is never identified.

Manage Your Fear and Anger

If you're surrounded and immobilized by excessive fear, step back again and think. No one is invincible. You *can* defeat the person who betrayed you. That doesn't mean you have the ability or right to hurt them or exact revenge. What it means is you *can* take the actions necessary to effectively cope with abuse and protect and remove yourself from any unhealthy relationship.

Fear, apprehension, and doubt are tools of the great adversary of God. They deplete faith and hope. On the other hand, belief in yourself and your ability to do tends to become a self-fulfilling prophecy. If you allow it to do so, fear can keep you in the box by immobilizing you. But with hope and belief in yourself, fear can be the motivator that gets you out. Break down the wall of fear that paralyzes you, that keeps you in the box. Let it induce you to seek help, sorting out what happened. Let it drive you to initiate a plan and take appropriate action to stop the continuing betrayal.

Dr. Jane Greer, a nationally renowned marriage and family therapist, states in her book, *Gridlock*, "How you chip away at that fear in spite of the crisis you may be facing can make the difference between attaining an effective and independent way of coping that affords you the attention, support, and resources you need and remaining gridlocked in a helpless, dependent mode." (Jane Greer, *Gridlock: Finding the Courage to Move on in Love, Work, and Life,* Doubleday, New York, 2000, p. 12, used by permission of the publisher.)

Anger, like fear, can be a positive or a negative motivator—negative if it persuades you to act recklessly and against your beliefs, positive if it drives you to prove your worth.

"When my clients can't see beyond their anger," says Dr. Greer in *How Could You Do This to Me?* "I often help them learn to manage it by explaining that anger is energy."

It can fuel you if you harness it in a positive way, like a car that uses gas to run. But if you flood the engine, it stalls out. In much the same way, when you're flooded with vengeful feelings, you become immobilized and can't move forward. You remain emotionally stuck, tied by an all-consuming obsession to the person who betrayed you. Hellbent on getting even, you spend so long in the role of victim that your energies are depleted and you miss vital opportunities for personal growth.

There is, however, one way in which revenge can be constructive: when it motivates you to prove your worth and prompts you to proclaim, like the character in the movie *Network,* "I'm mad

as hell, and I'm not going to take it anymore!"
When, in the aftermath of a betrayal of trust, you
begin to feel, "I count; I do matter"—and set out
to prove, to yourself and others, that you are
indeed worthy of love and trust—then, and only
then, can revenge be a positive force. (Jane Greer,
How Could You Do This to Me? Main Street
Books, New York, 1998, pp. 144-145, used by
permission of the publisher.)

Even though Martha accepted the separation from
her husband, the shock of discovering the extent of his
lies enraged her.

One evening, after another hearing but before the
divorce was signed and final, Martha sat on the couch
in the living room to relax and open the evening's mail.
There was a super-size envelope addressed to who she
thought was herself and her husband—*Mr. and Mrs....*
Some months before, the postmaster informed her that
ordinarily after a separation, the *Mr. and Mrs.* mail was
sent to the *Mr.* But because her husband had forged
her name on post office change-of-address cards, the
postmaster delivered the *Mr. and Mrs.* mail to her.
Looking at the document she removed from the large
envelope, Martha realized it was a marriage certificate
of her husband and another woman. The clerk's stamp
or seal was from a distant state.

Martha ran to the phone and called her brother.
Crying, she said, "You're not going to believe what I
have in my hand!"

After hearing about the contents of the envelope,
her brother rushed to her home with his scriptures in
hand. Believing he had her best interests at heart, he
cited scripture verses on forgiveness, and tried to
convince her to move forward by forgiving and
forgetting.

With tears rolling down her cheeks and her face reddened, Martha lifted her head and raised her hand. "Wait," she insisted, motioning for him to close the book. "Just let me be mad for a minute. Then I can probably hear what you have to say. But for now, just let me be mad!"

Handled appropriately, anger can produce energy that helps an individual:

- Process pain
- Resolve to change
- Determine a course of action
- Move forward with confidence and conviction

"Your brain is hard-wired to feel emotion. In the case of betrayal, you will feel anger," said Dorann C. Mitchell. "There's no reason to feel guilty about feeling angry. Healthy people feel emotions. But it is what they choose to do with those emotions that makes the difference." (Dorann C. Mitchell, in interview with Bettyanne Bruin.)

The key is to know that *getting* angry is okay, but *staying* angry is not. Uncontrolled anger leads to bitterness and revenge. Unchecked, anger, like fear, is self-destructive, immobilizing, and emotionally paralyzing.

Betrayal is what someone does to another person. Continuing to feel revengeful and angry is what the betrayed person does to himself or herself. Only the person betrayed can decide how much and for how long anger will be a part of his or her life. Staying angry keeps a person in the role of the victim and prevents the tough emotional work of healing and positive change. Staying angry actually keeps the betrayer in control of the betrayed.

Anger does not prevent future hurt, only action can do that. Martha's husband made wrong choices and

31

betrayed her. She had no control over his choices. She reacted with anger. That part of the equation, the anger, belonged to Martha. To exact satisfaction, Martha allowed her anger to confirm reality and fuel her determination to move forward with her life.

What is anger's greatest ally? Integrity. Even though an individual betrays another, the person betrayed has the choice to act responsibly, never compromising his or her integrity.

To channel anger constructively, the individual must gather the facts, not work from just hearsay and rememberings. Then, armed with the facts, he or she must decide a course of action to appropriately confront the betrayer.

There are times when people are genuinely unaware they have betrayed others. Confrontation can provide awareness for all individuals involved and potentially restore an important relationship that might otherwise be lost because of misunderstanding. On the other hand, confrontation of this kind might clarify for you the betrayer's true intentions and reveal disturbing thoughts and ideas. Use caution. Consider his or her attitude and explosive nature and your level of safety in determining what action you are going to take to confront the betrayer.

As mentioned in Chapter 1, Sarah consistently found porn sites on the history of her husband's computer. She hadn't totally ignored that fact. But when she questioned him, he said it was nothing to worry about. "It could actually be a tool to draw us closer," he remarked. "But since it bothers you, I won't do it again."

Over the years, Sarah found the resurfacing porn addresses increasingly disturbing. Going to Richard again, she addressed the issue. He responded in a remorseful tone. "I promise. I will *never* do this again."

The only problem was, this was at least the tenth

time he made such a promise. With each renewed promise, his remorseful attitude was more passionate and convincing to achieve what he ultimately desired (a living-a-lie life, a do-what-I-want-with-no-consequence life, a double life). And Sarah was so desirous to achieve what she ultimately wanted (a problem-free life) that together an unspoken choice was made to believe him, or at least leave the problem alone, and move forward in the relationship.

At last Sarah's conscience got the better of her and she decided to be more proactive in her efforts to eliminate the pornography problem. She began asking Richard questions like, *how, why, when, and where* did he engage in pornography *episodes*.

With each confrontation he became more resistant and defiant, accusing her of not trusting him, saying his problems were behind him. The discussions easily and quickly became heated, emphasizing her lack of trust instead of his failure to keep promises. The result was always the same, a hands-off stalemate, until she discovered the pornographic teen sites.

Thinking he was now dabbling in illegal activities, Sarah called the state attorney general's office to report what she found. She was informed that his viewing was not illegal, as *teen,* in this case, meant over the age of eighteen. But, her husband's defiant attitude and conscious choice to continue his addiction became too upsetting to ignore, especially since they had three teenage daughters living at home.

"This pornography use has to stop," she said to her husband. With this demand, Sarah's journey from discovery into the real world of betrayal began.

Counseling did not improve the situation and repeated confrontations proved futile. Their relationship unraveled as Richard became more belligerent, still insisting Sarah had the problem, not him. He became oppressive toward her, coming home from work unexpectedly, literally tiptoeing into the room and surprising her in the middle of the day. Then proclaiming (when there was no cause) that he had reason to check in on her to make sure she wasn't having an affair. He suggested to their friends that Sarah might be dealing with a problem of male addiction. At the same time, he became more and more combative and resistant to questions about his past, present, or future.

Sarah insisted she needed some time and space. Richard moved out. Now feeling safe, she searched the house while Richard filed for divorce. Sarah cleaned closets, drawers, and file cabinets in an attempt to gather information and rid the house of unseemly materials. She was shocked at what she found— countless computer and hard copy files of hardcore pornography, information proving years and years of strip-joint activities, other women, and huge financial improprieties.

"How could I have allowed this to happen?" she chided herself. "Was I blind? How can Richard do this to me? How could the porn be more important than I am?"

Friends, church leaders, and professionals tried to convince her that what Richard did was not against her, but part of a lifelong problem he had. But their words did little to ease her mind. "I was mad at myself, and angry with him," she said.

Still in betrayal mode, Richard tried to convince Sarah that she was the one with the bigger problem— the inability to show unconditional love. But Sarah knew genuine love was never meant to include embracing evil. No longer would she allow "love" to include behaviors that went against her basic values and beliefs.

Was facing reality painful? "You bet it was," Sarah

states. "The world as I knew it came to an abrupt end. And it was now on my shoulders to create a new one. I remember sitting alone in the living room one day," she recalls. "I felt nearly overtaken by my anger and regrets. But I didn't want to be that way. At one point I said out loud, 'Okay, this is where I'm at. Now where am I going from here?'"

A pivotal point is reached when an individual lets go of what he or she cannot change, accepts the choices of others, and fully accepts and acknowledges his or her own reality. It's almost as though a divergence in the road is made possible through acceptance—one course being anger and revenge, the other being the first step toward hope and a renewal of happiness. Certainly it is a pivotal point to finding peace. The past is the past and cannot be replaced. But each person does have control over his or her future and the choices ahead.

The second step—Acceptance

Accept and acknowledge your reality, and take responsibility for your future.

I accept the reality of:

CHAPTER THREE

The Third Step—Action

Strong reasons make strong actions.
—William Shakespeare

"This pornography use has to stop," Sarah said to her husband, finally accepting her reality and facing her fears. Confronting him, she solidly stood her ground, her actions based on a new commitment to her personal value system.

To take appropriate action, you must know what is important to you—what your priorities are—what you believe in. Do you know *your* personal values? What values will you stand firmly to defend?

An old Rwandan proverb states, "You can outdistance that which is running after you, but not what is running inside you." (Sophie Bevan, *The Gift of Inner Peace,* Ryland, Peters & Small, London, England, 2004, p. 21, used by permission of the publisher.)

Do not let your fears and anger drive your actions. The key that unlocks the lid and gives you the power to climb out of your box is knowing and believing in yourself. You can get even with the person who betrayed you, not by revenge, but by standing up for yourself, by blocking the continual betrayal. Purposely allow your standards and integrity, even your willingness to conform to God's will, to be reflected in the selections of what you say and what you do.

What, then, are your personal values and priorities? As psychologist Dr. Richard L. Williams, author of *Tell Me How I'm Doing,* has said, "Personal values are at the central core of who we are and what we ultimately become. Our values include such basic character elements as honesty, integrity, respect, trustworthiness, truthfulness, and hope. Many of our values were formed as children and were highly influenced by our parents. Other personal values are defined as we make our choices throughout our lives. The better choices and behaviors we make the more wholesome values we tend to form. Likewise, the poorer choices and behaviors we make the less wholesome values we tend to form. As adults it's critically important, therefore, to make wise choices followed up with appropriate actions, because that process goes a long way toward defining personal values." (Richard L. Williams, personal communication with Fay Klingler.)

What do *you* stand for? Truth? Fidelity? What values or beliefs would you list that frame your code of conduct? Do you honor and respect the divine role you have as a child of God? Do you pride yourself in a high work ethic? Perhaps you believe you should respect people and property. Maybe you would say, "I stand for fair treatment of all individuals I come in contact with. And I expect them to reciprocate, treating me with value, respect, and honesty."

Your attitudes and values help determine your view of the betraying behavior. Often they are the deciding factors in how you respond to your circumstances and the outcome of your life. Sometimes the hardest part of realizing a change for the better in relationships is believing you have the power to bring about that change.

And sometimes you just can't see a realistic starting point.

My personal beliefs and values are:

_____

_____

_____

_____

_____

_____

_____

_____

_____

_____

_____

_____

_____

_____

_____

Begin by defining your beliefs and values. Then determine what you want from the relationship. Let's use the simple example of Emily introduced in Chapter 1. She's the editor who was taken advantage of by her writer friend. Emily's code of conduct was based on her belief and expectation of fairness—she would provide a service to Ann, and Ann would reciprocate with an equally valuable service. When it became apparent there was no equity and that Ann was not going to keep her word and pay for the additional service, Emily stopped cooperating with Ann. "It was a disappointment," she said, "but I had to stop allowing Ann to take advantage of me. It wasn't fair."

Like Sarah, based on her beliefs and values, Emily reached a limit of tolerance. Ann's obvious choice to be unfair was the factor for Emily's eventual decision not to cooperate further and for her negative opinion of the relationship. "I would like to have been close friends with Ann," Emily remarked. "But close friends aren't just users."

Choose to Act

Avoid belittling yourself if you've failed to pick up on the clues of the betrayer. Don't label yourself or call yourself names. Don't say, "How could I have been so stupid? Am I dumb? I should have seen that!"

Betrayers can be experts at manipulation, subtlety, and promoting confusion, as in the case of attorney and congresswoman, Enid Greene Waldholtz, who was duped by her chameleon husband, Joe. He presented himself as a wealthy, generous, caring man, when in reality he obtained his wealth by stealing from his family. And within twenty-one months of marriage he practiced his craft on Enid, embezzling her campaign funds and *borrowing* four million dollars from her father. From the beginning, members of her family held Joe suspect. At one point, Enid's brother-in-law even called Enid's father and asked if he wanted him to "check out Joe." There was a slight pause; then her father answered, "Oh no, Jim, we don't do that. The Greenes don't do that." (Lee Benson, *Blind Trust: The True Story of Enid Greene and Joe Waldholtz,* Agreka Books, Scottsdale, AZ, 1997, pp. 261-62, used by permission of the author.)

As Joe's fraudulent actions became evident, many individuals realized they had been taken in by his charade. Looking back, Jim thought it might not have been such a bad idea to have investigated Joe before Enid married him. Jim "knew, as everyone in the family knew, that they all could have asked more questions, they all could have been more skeptical. In hindsight there were signs any of them could have picked up on.

"Joe's fraud was always there, just below the surface, and no one had dipped underneath to see what lurked below." (Benson, *Blind Trust,* p. 269.)

As soon as he met Joe, Chuck Roistacher, a member of Enid's legal defense team, recognized a pattern "that was common to all con men: Always tell the truth, just don't tell the whole truth. Tell just enough, five percent, ten percent at most, to wedge your foot in the door and deflect the issue, but no more. Tell just enough to establish a front of credibility and keep up your facade.

"The clarity of hindsight showed just how adept Joe had been at the partial truth, at wrapping a lie in just enough fact that the whole package seemed genuine. With that tactic, he'd taken Enid—and everyone around her—on a very expensive...ride." (Benson, *Blind Trust,* p. 296.)

In Chapter 1 you were advised to stop denying something is wrong—to see things as they really are. In Chapter 2 you were asked to look outside your box and find answers to help clarify and accept the problem. This is not the time to beat yourself up for failing to recognize and face the problem earlier. Whatever happened to you has happened to others. They have learned to cope, and so must you. Instead of blaming, believe in yourself and your abilities. Use your strengths to buoy yourself up and take action. And that action must be consistent with your code of conduct. Inner peace comes as you maintain and act upon your values: integrity, morality, accountability, and so forth.

"The truth is," says Dr. Jane Greer, "when you fail to play an active role in your own life, the problems don't go away; they go underground and inevitably crop up later." (*Gridlock*, p. 19, used by permission of the publisher.)

Act—don't just react. Of course your choice of action will be determined partly by the response you receive from the person who betrayed you. And this might mean there will be a confrontation, a difficult move for some individuals. First, however, you must choose what values you are going to defend and what you want from the relationship.

As you contemplate confronting this person, ask yourself, "What do I really want; what are my options? What do I want for myself? For him or her? For my family?" Of course you want to be happy and successful. But what does happy and successful really mean to you?

From my point of view, my options are:

_____

_____

_____

_____

_____

_____

_____

_____

_____

_____

_____

_____

_____

_____

_____

_____

_____

Let's say you've determined your husband is having an affair with another woman. You can't change the fact that it happened. From this point, what do you really want? Would you be satisfied if he chose to break off the affair and commit to be faithful to you? Or has he already gone past your limit of tolerance and you will only be happy with divorce? If you think you want revenge, is that consistent with your values, your code of conduct? Probably not. What do you really want from this relationship now? In the future?

For myself, I really want now:

_____

_____

_____

_____

_____

_____

_____

_____

_____

_____

_____

_____

_____

_____

In the future:

_____

_____

_____

_____

_____

_____

_____

_____

_____

_____

_____

_____

_____

Making an *I want...*list can, to some extent, help you process the pain and see your situation in a more realistic perspective. Also, specifying what you want for the other person, again consistent with your values, causes your brain to be in gear, not just your emotions. Depending on the offense, coming up with what you want for the other person can be a difficult task, but it is possible. Just be sure that your expectations in the relationship are appropriate and practical.

Using the example above, perhaps you wish for your husband to genuinely renew his love for you, with his heart loyal and committed. You want him to be able to forgive himself for the bad choice he made. On the other hand, you might want for him to be able to control his temper when you confront him—to bow out in a gentlemanly manner—to leave without making a fuss.

For him or her, I really want now:

_____

_____

_____

_____

_____

_____

_____

_____

_____

In the future:

_____

_____

_____

_____

_____

_____

_____

_____

Remember Todd, discussed in Chapter 2? For himself, he wanted his wife to be loyal to him. For them both, he wanted her to be faithful to the religious beliefs he thought their marriage was based on.

"It is my thought," said Todd, "that the way we chose to live our religious principles diverged at some point. And we mutually became our own worst enemies in repairing that divergence. I felt frustrated and alone the more Jan, in my mind, chose to sit on the edge of obedience to the commandments, and she felt increasingly guilty living around me because of the way I responded to those choices. It is difficult for anyone to live in circumstances where they have made mistakes, and those around them show more discontent than understanding."

Todd did not choose to separate and divorce. That was Jan's decision. "Constantly I fought for Jan, doing anything I could to win back her heart. I gave flowers. I identified and did things she wanted. But this usually backfired, turning her off even more," he lamented.

Together they visited a psychiatrist, who had been recommended to them. "Then he asked to see us separately, and eventually he hoped to bring us back together. That, however, never happened," said Todd. "In my session with him, he taught me to re-evaluate my foundations. Human nature was too frail to be that foundation. If love was to be my foundation, and it failed, where would I be? He taught me that the Savior was the only sure foundation." That foundation, the basis of Todd's beliefs and values, remained solid.

So first, you want to determine your position by answering the following questions:

- What do you stand for—what values are you going to defend?
- What do you perceive are your options?
- What do you want for yourself?
- What do you want for the other person?

Once you have answered these questions, if it is safe, you can confront the other person directly to hold him or her accountable for what has occurred.

Confronting Your Betrayer

The response to your confrontation will help you choose your actions. *If it is safe* is a major consideration, however. Betrayers are often secretive, manipulative, and intimidating. Some are also unpredictable and violent. Carefully assess the nature of the betrayal and the temperament of the betrayer. Trust your gut—your instinct—that gnawing feeling turned positive. If you suspect the other person may not be able to control their reaction and temper, do not confront him or her, at least not alone. Act instead on the information you have gathered from sources outside the box.

If one of your options is to attempt to reconcile the relationship, or if you want to step inside the box to get a first-hand look at the betrayer's explanation for his or her behavior, confrontation can be a healthy and confirming move. Confrontation *does not* mean hostile defiance or forced physical conflict. Confrontation *does* mean meeting face to face to present the facts as you understand them for acknowledgment and examination.

In preparation for this meeting, put in writing the specific information you have discovered regarding the betrayal. Not the hearsay and rumors, but the facts. Write down the facts you gathered. If claims are made to the contrary, and the tension of the moment causes you to feel confused, this information will act as your reality checklist. Those written items are what you focus the meeting on, not what the betrayer attempts to distract your attention to.

I discovered:

_____

_____

_____

_____

_____

_____

_____

_____

_____

_____

_____

_____

_____

_____

_____

_____

Before confronting the betrayer, consider the following:

- What do I want from the confrontation?
- Where will I confront?
- When will I confront?
- How will I confront; what will I say?
- How will I evaluate the confrontation?

Consider What You Want From the Confrontation

If you'll only settle for an apology and a quick show of amends, you're going to be disappointed. But if you're looking for the opportunity to express your findings and your feelings and learn from the betrayer's response, you'll be rewarded. Look at this as the opportunity to learn new information, to see the issues from a different perspective, or to confirm what you already know. Ask yourself, "Is there any chance I misunderstood or misinterpreted the information I've gathered?" You are after a discovery of the betrayer's attitude and whether he or she will talk openly and honestly with you. Be curious. Listen. Keep your brain in gear.

Consider Where You Will Confront

In what environment could you expect the most cooperation from the betrayer? Where and under what circumstances is he or she most likely to feel safe to speak openly? The bedroom and the car are not options. The bedroom causes a conflict of thought in critical conversations. And being in a moving car while discussing something this intense would be risky.

Weather permitting, is there a location outside that lends itself to your needs? Or perhaps your living room or kitchen would serve the purpose. The location needs to be someplace where you both can sit down, if desired, and where background noises won't disturb the conversation.

If there is any possible threat to your safety, do not confront the betrayer alone. Invite a friend, relative, or ecclesiastical leader to be with you. Your friend or leader offers a buffer of protection. Also, because your friend is more objective in this situation, he or she may pick up on subtle body language and words that you miss. While you may be caught up in emotion and busy trying to figure out what to say and how to interpret responses, your friend can listen and watch carefully with an assignment to remember and later relate what actually occurs.

Often you cannot effectively anticipate how the betrayer will respond to the information you present. So always imagine a worst-case scenario and plan accordingly. Design a pathway for escape in the event the meeting becomes dangerous. If indoors, use a room where there is access to an outside exit.

Consider meeting with a counselor or with your church leader at his or her location. Often these individuals have training or experience to help facilitate open dialogue, and the neutral site can provide a safe environment.

If there are children involved, take them to a safe area prior to the meeting where they will not witness the confrontation. Having the children away from the location minimizes any pressure the betrayer might feel, one way or the other, to act to impress them. It also diminishes their use as targets in verbal or physical threats.

Consider When You Will Confront

Ask to meet when both of you are reasonably calm, not as an immediate follow-up to an argument, nor right after the other person has exploded from getting a traffic ticket. Meet after you have eaten a full meal, avoiding hunger as a factor in the response. Propose to meet at a time when neither of you expect to be interrupted by someone coming for an appointment, and at a time when you do not have to leave to go elsewhere. Plan ample free time to discuss the issues.

Consider How You Will Confront—
What You Will Say

When the stakes are high in a conversation, fear and emotion play a huge part in what is said and not said—fear of not saying the right things, fear of not saying things the right way, fear of the inability to control yourself in the situation. Two distinct actions are requisite.

Beforehand, get on your knees and ask God for help. Ask for discernment. "What should I say? How should I say it? And please help me be calm, think clearly, and be able to judge in a proper light what I see and hear. Please direct me to act in a righteous manner." Ask specifically that you not be deceived by yourself or by the other person. *Then consciously be sensitive to the power of God and what He might want you to do, and trust your judgment.*

Second, deliberately step back from your fear and emotion. Kerry Patterson, Joseph Grenny, Ron McMillan, and Al Switzler in their book, *Crucial Conversations,* write,

> When your emotions start cranking up, key brain functions start shutting down. Not only do you prepare to take flight, but your peripheral vision actually narrows. In fact, when you feel genuinely threatened, you can scarcely see beyond what's right in front of you. Similarly, when you feel the outcome of a conversation is being threatened, you have a hard time seeing beyond the point you're trying to make. By pulling yourself out of the content of an argument and watching for fear, you reengage your brain and your full vision returns." (Patterson, Grenny, McMillan, and Switzler, *Crucial Conversations: Tools for Talking When Stakes are High,* McGraw-Hill, New York, 2002, p. 45, used by permission of the publisher.)

Get your brain in gear so you observe and act instead of just react. If you remain focused on the fear or the anger, your emotions will do your talking for you, and you will fail to hear what is actually said. You will only hear what sustains your suspicions, even if the real intent of the other person is innocent.

As you begin the meeting, ask yourself again, "Is it possible there could be a rational explanation for what happened?" For this meeting, purposely set your emotions aside.

Practice what you're going to say in front of an audience—facing a mirror, or in front of a trusted friend or relative, a counselor, a church leader. Or perhaps you might recite your message into a tape recorder. Listen to your recording, or ask your friend to repeat back to you what you said. Remember, it's not so much what you say that counts but what the other person hears. All things considered, if you were the betrayer and the facts were presented in this way, how would you react?

Asking "Why did you do this?" of a betrayer is often useless and might only serve to confuse the issue. Betrayers don't always know why they act and react in a certain manner. If they do, they're seldom willing to share the truth of the matter. Their motives are generally self-serving. They do not necessarily act on logic and reason. If forced to explain *why,* a fabricated *truth* could prevent you from focusing on his or her acknowledgement of the betrayal. Finding out the *why* may forever be a mystery left in the hands of God.

You wrote down the facts you discovered about the betrayal. You wrote down what you stand for, what you believe your options are, what you really want for yourself, and what you really want for the other person. As mentioned before, these written items are your focus.

Begin the meeting by telling the other person what you *don't* want. "I don't want to argue with you about..." "I don't want you to think that I don't appreciate how hard you work to..." "I'm not trying to..." Then state what you *do* want. "But I do want to hear your explanation of..." "My only goal is to..." "I do want us to be able to talk so that we can understand each other about..." "What I really want is to

52

genuinely…" "I want to understand your point of view about…"

Now state your discovery in the form of facts and ask the other person to explain. Don't exaggerate by throwing in phrases like "you always," "you never," or "everyone has told me everything."

Dr. Richard L. Williams said, "Many well meaning people use the words *always* or *never* inappropriately when describing something bothersome or frustrating. They might say 'You *always* do that,' or 'You *never* do anything my way.' In most cases, statements such as these are overstated and technically inaccurate, so they usually inflame the conversation with unnecessary feelings, which often leads to an argument." (Richard L. Williams, *Coaching Strategies to Improve Performance*, Vision Publishing Company, Sandy, Utah, 1999, p. 70, used by permission.)

Use appropriate body language and maintain eye-to-eye contact. Avoid arrogant or haughty gestures. Actions, like words, speak for themselves. Deliver your message clearly and concisely, holding the other person responsible, not only for the information he or she is receiving, but for the way in which he or she receives it.

Be careful, however, to match your voice tone with your well-chosen words. If your tone of voice is anxious, defensive, or hostile, the other person will ignore your words and respond to the tone. If you're worried about your words and your tone of voice sending a mixed message and the other person not receiving what you intended, call attention to it and explain what your voice tone is saying. "I know I sound angry, but that's because I'm nervous and this matter is very important to me." Clarifying what your tone is saying decreases the chances of the other person becoming offended.

Observe Quietly

Now look at the other person and listen for the response. This means you are quiet. This means you are observant of his or her body language. This means you are focused on your objective—not to argue, but to receive and interpret the information offered by the betrayer.

Especially watch the other person's attitude. Is he or she apologetic and remorseful? "Oh, I'm so sorry about that. I didn't intend to hurt you." Or is the other person angry and blaming? "How'd you find out about that? I wouldn't have had to do that if you would have…"

Does he or she acknowledge the facts you have uncovered to be true? Are reasonable answers given for reasonable questions? (If a realistic and sincere *why* of what happened comes out in the explanation, count it a bonus!) Or does the other person attempt to play with your mind by twisting the truth or insulting or making fun of you to divert your attention away from discussing what happened? Does he or she work a fragment of truth in a circle of lies?

Depending on the relationship, the other person may know your vulnerable points better than you do. For some time, he or she has probably been taking advantage of your weaknesses to inspire you with the idea that you are no good, always wrong, prone to make mistakes, or dependent on him or her. If so, do not believe the manipulative behavior and become confused and emotional. Force your brain to stay in gear. Think about what you really want. Go back to your reality checklist.

If a contrite explanation is offered and you want further clarification, ask specific questions that help you see a broader view of what happened and determine if change is possible. Lay aside your pride. Watch your attitude. Be careful that your tone of voice doesn't indicate you have already made a conclusion. Lean on God for discernment, keeping in mind the betrayer's explanation may not qualify to be taken at face value (as you most likely have been in the habit of doing). At this point, what is said is not trustworthy unless it matches what has been done. If you sense something's amiss, probe further.

Set Reasonable Limits

The other person may choose to deny your discovery with a response like, "That's a lie. I didn't do that. You're just trying to make me look bad." If so, don't add to the problem by defending your position and producing a fight. Try to remain calm. You don't need to *win* in this confrontation. You don't need to prove your point. The betrayer knows the truth, and you know it; he or she is just playing a mind game. Don't let yourself be sucked into a negative circle of discussion.

Instead, restate what you do not want and what you do want. Tell the other person, "This discussion is not to prove a point. I already have proof of the matter." Once again, ask for an explanation.

If the betrayer's response becomes belligerent, don't withdraw (unless your physical safety is at risk). Stand your ground. State the person's name, "(Jim), I want to hear your explanation of what happened."

If the person is yelling and not allowing you to restate your request, attempt to interrupt him or her by saying his or her name again. Say it in a matter-of-fact sort of way, without fear or anger. You may need to say the name over and over and over again before you get his or her attention. "Jim, Jim, Jim. Excuse me, Jim." If the other person raises his or her voice to prevent you from speaking, continue anyway. When you get the other person's attention, state, "It appears discussing this topic is uncomfortable for you. Please help me understand your position about this."

Set limits for yourself when dealing with the other person's anger. If he or she persists in combative behavior, tell him or her, "I hoped to hear your side of the story—your explanation of what happened. Your unwillingness to talk in a reasonable manner forces me to come to my own conclusions." Then ask the person to leave the premises until he or she can cool down. Tell the other person that if he or she has a change of heart and chooses to talk, you are available to listen.

Consider How You Will Evaluate the Confrontation

The result of this type of confrontation will bring you to a new level of acceptance. You must accept the other person's choice of whether to cooperate or not. You must accept his or her response mode. In this case, acceptance also means no more giving in, ignoring, or tolerating unreasonable behavior. It means showing respect for yourself and standing your ground. It means taking responsibility for what you have allowed and will continue to allow to happen. It means letting the other person be responsible for and own what he or she has chosen to do and will choose to do in the future.

Expand your reality checklist. Write down what you believe occurred in the meeting. Compare your new checklist with your values list and your "I want..." list. From what you heard and observed in the confrontation, are your options any different than what you imagined before the confrontation? Is there room for compromise? Did the other person confirm the facts and broaden your view? Is reconciliation an option, or does staying in the relationship go against what you believe? You are now the deciding factor. The ball, so to speak, is in your court. What action are you going to take?

Don't jump to conclusions too quickly, but don't be ambivalent about making decisions and acting on them either. Look honestly at yourself and at the other person. If you see a chance for reconciliation, what are the terms? For you? For the other person? Can trust be rebuilt?

Caution. You must value yourself enough to stand independently, regardless of your desire to be loved, to belong. You can no longer be dependent on the other person's attention or feedback. *Don't allow yourself to retreat back into an abusive relationship. Act with new awareness.*

To help you judge, look back. Consider how you have felt about the relationship over time. Don't distort or revise what happened in the past to satisfy yourself today. Acknowledge what was honestly good or bad. Were you ever happy with the other person? Did you feel safe? Can you remember what brought the two of you together? The future of the relationship may partly hinge on the strength of those early experiences. If your relationship was strong and positive in the beginning— meaning that you both tried to manage conflict constructively, shared loving feelings and common goals, had mutually satisfying sex, and enjoyed a reasonable number of fulfilling activities together—there may be hope. However, if you cannot find much to build on— meaning the relationship rarely worked, intimidation and fear seemed to rule—then the relationship may not be salvageable today.

When the attitude and response of the other person gives you hope for the relationship and a reason to grant it some time, make clear to the other person what you want for yourself and what you want for him or her. Explain your new boundaries. You don't have to threaten or go into great detail like, "If you go into the other room to make your phone calls, I'll know something is up, and I'll leave you!"

Generally state what you can't tolerate, and ask the other person to respect and honor your needs. "Under the circumstances, I will have to work at trusting your fidelity. So please don't give me any reason to suspect you are keeping secrets."

Perhaps you need some additional space to help you sort things out. At any rate, there is room for both of you to change. You both must exercise your agency to make the relationship work. And you both must cultivate a healthy climate for talking, so you can agree on a shared purpose and specific goals.

Successful change happens best when it is broken into small increments. Simplify. Concentrating on the basics, focus on one or two specific changes at a time. You might benefit by giving this window of opportunity a time frame before you re-evaluate—six weeks, six months, a year. Then pray like it all depends on God, and work like it all depends on you. This doesn't mean you work to make things that are still wrong look and feel good. And it doesn't mean you stretch your boundaries to accommodate the other person's actions. What it does mean is that you firmly defend your values and do your part, and give the other person full agency to fulfill his or her part of the agreement.

Now that you are both carrying the ball, each of you must accept an appropriate share of responsibility for what went wrong and for what now goes right or wrong. It comes down to choices—your choice to respect and stand up for yourself, and the other person's choice to put the relationship first and sincerely travel with you to a place of increased hope, healing, and a new beginning.

Just because you make changes doesn't mean he or she is automatically going to make changes. And certainly you might not always be in sync with each other. Patience is a virtue. Only you can decide when patience has been stretched too far and courage to act in another direction is called for. You use the other person's actions once again to measure the relationship—not endless promises to take action and change, but real change. The other person's words must be substantiated by his or her actions. Have faith in your ability to make good decisions, and act appropriately on those decisions.

Whitney, married sixteen years, chose to stay in her marriage, even after discovering her husband had an affair with another woman. He chose to break off the affair and attempt to rebuild the relationship with his wife. When she was asked, "How do you mend and go on?" Whitney replied, "At times, it is *so* hard and the relationship is *so* fragile."

If anything, a wife who stays has to get to a point where she can trust her husband again. And it can take such a long time to get to this point! But you *have* to, because a relationship cannot thrive forever without trust.

For us, we had to take baby steps. For him, he had to understand my mistrust of him. For me, I had to experiment with trusting him again, because I knew that the more I showed I trusted him, the more he felt at ease to be open with me. If I continued endlessly to watch every little thing he did, he would not be able to endear himself to me. And the more a spouse trusts his or her spouse, the more that spouse will feel trustworthy. Time is the biggest factor and a lot of work on behalf of both parties. Even after ten years, recently, we had a situation that showed me, for one of the first times, how much he has really changed and is now truly and appropriately and emotionally intimate with me. He came to me and held me in his arms. He looked me in the eyes, told me he loved me, and said that he wanted to spend the rest of his life with me.

Because initiating this type of positive, emotionally intimate behavior was such a new approach for him, I'm embarrassed to admit that my first reaction was to think in my mind, *Why is he doing this? What has he been up to now?* All of these thoughts flooded through my mind. But I didn't say any of them. Instead, I looked at him and said sincerely, "Really? Is this how you really feel?"

He didn't say much at the time, but two days later he came to me and said, "I want you to know that the other night when I told you how much I loved you, you really hurt me when you questioned my sincerity. I really *do* love you."

I was shocked. Never had he pondered upon such thoughts like this before. To come to me two days later, instead of taking his thoughts elsewhere, and tell me of his vulnerable concerns and be able to share them with me and seek for more understanding, told me that his thoughts and feelings for me are genuine.

Expect it to take time, possibly lots of time, patience, and discernment. But it is possible. And it can be worth the investment!

Try Again

When the attitude and response of the other person dissolves your hope for the relationship, but you feel you must explain your position and give him or her one last chance, tell the other person the ball is in his or her court. "You have the power to win or loose this game. It is up to you."

Explain again what you don't want. "I don't want us to separate. I don't want our relationship to fail." Tell him or her what you do want. "I want a relationship with open communication, a relationship where we share values and goals, where we both feel respected and safe." Now be specific. "To me, that means…" Say what isn't working and offer an alternative behavior. Be tentative, clear, and concise, without displaying emotion.

You don't need to go on and on with your explanation. Just state again the values you are defending, give this trial period a timetable (either verbally or in your mind), and leave it at that.

The other person now has the choice to either accept your request and move in your direction, or continue down the same path following the same patterns as before. And you must be prepared. It's not like you're automatically expecting the relationship to fail. But you must resolve to follow through with a determined consequence if the other person does not act appropriately.

When Martha confronted her husband about the hidden debts and the welfare fraud, she stated, "Just tell me the truth and we'll put all this behind us and go forward with a clean slate."

He responded with, "I can't do that!"

When she asked him, "Where is your integrity?" he answered emphatically, "I *am* honest!"

His answers did not match what she knew to be true. "I was hurt. I wanted so much for the marriage to remain intact. But I didn't want to be lied to any more. I felt I had to take action and make a responsible choice for myself and for my children." Martha filed for divorce.

There's an old saying, "The person shooting the bullet isn't the person feeling the pain." Sometimes, in the case of betrayal, the other person feels no need to change until he or she emotionally connects with a just consequence and feels some of the pain he or she has created.

Ultimately, you are powerless to control the other person's decisions, emotions, or actions. So you act to the best of your ability to control *yourself.*

Ensure Your Safety

There is a difference between consistent violent or disruptive behavior and an occasional temper tantrum. At the time of confrontation, the other person is not necessarily going to suddenly change and be reasonable. If the betrayer's behavioral patterns are predictably violent, or enough so that you fear for the safety of your children or yourself, do not attempt to confront him or her without taking appropriate preventative measures to ensure your protection. A violent person seldom recognizes his or her abusive actions as destructive choices. He or she simply acts without thinking, on impulse, with no check on behavior.

According to the National Coalition Against Domestic Violence (NCADV), "Leaving is the most dangerous time in the abusive cycle and should be planned with caution." They suggest the following:

- Think of possible escape routes and practice how you and your children can get out safely.
- Choose a code word to use with family, friends, and neighbors when you need the police.
- Talk to your children about keeping themselves safe by hiding or going to a neighbor's house *and not protecting you.*

- Try to think of safe places to go if you have to leave in a hurry—a friend, family, coworker, shelter.
- Call a domestic violence hotline or local shelter to learn about the laws and other resources *before* you need them. To find out about the domestic violence services in your community, contact the National Domestic Violence Hotline—800-799-SAFE (800-799-7233)—or www.ndvh.org.
- Use your judgment and learn to trust your instinct. No one knows better than you how dangerous the situation can get.

Martha mentioned her husband's history of abusive actions and her concern for the safety of her children in Chapter 1. Remember, she said, "At one point in our marriage, I realized it wasn't safe to leave the children with him. He was so unpredictably explosive. So I tried not to go out in the evenings, once he came home."

Because of that history, prior to confronting him with divorce papers, she was given the address of a government safe house, where she and the children could retreat at a moment's notice. She was warned at all times to have clothing and personal items for herself and her children in the trunk of her car, enough to get them by for two or three days, in the event they had to leave in a hurry.

The risk of harm does not diminish immediately after separation from an abusive partner. Bureau of Justice statistics show that "separated women are 3 times more likely than divorced women and 25 times more likely than married women to be victims of violence at the hands of an intimate partner." (Ronet Bachman and Linda Salzman, *Violence Against Women: Estimates From the Redesigned Survey*, NCADV, 2000, used with permission.)

The NCADV warns that "in 1994, approximately 37% of women seeking injury-related treatment in hospital emergency rooms were there because of injuries inflicted by a current or former spouse or intimate partner. (Michael Rand, *Violence-Related Injuries Treated in Hospital Emergency Room Departments*, NCADV, 1997, p. 5, used with permission.)

Don't expose yourself to greater danger by failing to take appropriate actions. How are you equipped to deal with retribution from the betrayer? What is your safety plan?

To be safe, I will:

_____

_____

_____

_____

_____

_____

_____

_____

_____

_____

_____

_____

_____

Kami was a single mom of two children when she met Jeff. After their marriage, they moved to a neutral home some distance from her family, "and he suddenly turned," she recalled.

He became physically, mentally, and verbally abusive. He tried choking me on several occasions, left bruises all over my body and face. When he left the house, he would disconnect the phone lines outside so I could not call for help. He took the only vehicle we had so I could not leave. One time, he even tried to run me over with his car. And he tried to run us both off the road into a ditch.

I am one who is a firm believer that everything happens for a reason. So I thought perhaps all of this was happening to help me grow as a person, to make me stronger, so I could handle greater challenges God had in store for me. I was grasping for answers, though, and was trying my best to understand why my world tumbled, and why this man who claimed to love me hurt me so badly. It was my believing that there was a reason for it all (despite the fact that I did not know what the reason was) that helped me stay strong through it all.

I tried to confront Jeff about the problem, but he denied there was one, and got defensive and abusive again. I managed to flee once and went to a mutual friend's home. I had never (before this) told anyone about the situation. So this time, having made someone else aware of the problem, Jeff realized I meant business (or so I thought). The mutual friend tried talking to him, explaining that what he was doing was wrong and that he needed help.

I said to Jeff, "People don't hurt people, especially those they supposedly care about." I told him I was afraid he was going to seriously hurt me or even kill me if he didn't get help. He cried and begged me to come back. I did, under the assumption he would get help. Peace lasted about one week, and then Jeff went right back to the same behavior, this time making sure he threatened me about not going to our friends again.

I seriously feared for my life. I prayed for me and for him to get the help he truly needed. I prayed for the courage to stand my ground on how I should be treated with respect and love. It did not take too long to realize Jeff was just not capable of providing that. I felt I had no choice but to seek safety for me and my kids and leave him. I used the emotional strength I gained during the eight months of abuse, and ran for safety.

Kami's home was in Pennsylvania, but her job was in Manhattan. Her husband drove her to and from work every day. "One day, once Jeff's car left my workplace," she explained, "I called my sister and asked her to come get me. She took me to the police station and the courthouse where I filed an order of protection."

In the meantime, Kami's husband called and found she was not at work. So he went to the school and made up a story, telling the teachers he was picking up the children for doctors' appointments. He called her cell phone and left messages. "He had the kids say hello on the phone to prove to me that he had them, and that was his way of forcing me to deal with him," Kami said.

Then, with a police escort, she went to her home to see if Jeff was there. He was not. "So the officer allowed me and my sister to go in and gather some belongings. Just as we were about to go on a hunt to find Jeff, we saw his car up the road. In my sister's car, my sister and I approached the vehicle with the officer, in his car, behind us. Once Jeff saw the police car, he did not resist giving up the children and being served the order of protection."

Kami and her children moved in with her sister until they could get a place of their own. And she filed for divorce. But the abuse did not stop there. "He stalked me, harassed me, followed me everywhere," she said. "It continued for over a year. He used my name to incur debt and damaged my property.

"I again tried to see the situation as a test—a test of faith, a test of courage, a test of will. I did not know why it was happening. It was beyond my comprehension. I just believed it was happening to me for a specific reason. Maybe even to help Jeff in some way. At any rate, I had to stand tall and stop this man from doing these brutal things to me."

Kami had to courageously walk away from the abusive relationship.

Thomas S. Monson, Second Counselor in the First Presidency of the Church of Jesus Christ of Latter-day Saints, said, "It is this sweet assurance that can guide you and me—in our time, in our day, in our lives. Of course, we will face fear, experience ridicule, and meet opposition. Let us have the courage to defy the consensus, the courage to stand for principle. Courage, not compromise, brings the smile of God's approval. Courage becomes a living and an attractive virtue when it is regarded not only as a willingness to die manfully, but as the determination to live decently...Remember that all men have their fears, but those who face their fears with dignity have courage as well." (Thomas S. Monson, "Courage Counts," *Ensign,* November 1986, The Church of Jesus Christ of Latter-day Saints, Salt Lake City, Utah, p. 40, used with permission.)

Jill, a runner, who also suffered the devastating effects of betrayal, compared her betrayer to a pebble.

"I was out running one morning, and one shoe flipped a small pebble into the other. The pebble, no larger than a small pea, began to irritate my foot as it worked its way under the heel, under the arch, then under the ball of my foot, where it remained lodged. I didn't want to slow down and stop running to remove the pebble (like confronting my betrayer). I thought, *Surely I can withstand a small pebble.* But after a short distance, I realized if I continued without facing the problem, I was consciously choosing to end my run with a hole in my sock and a raw, sore place on my foot. Either way, I was in charge of the choice, and I was in charge of the outcome. I finally stopped and took out the pebble—I accepted responsibility for my reality and acted upon it."

For some people, change is very difficult, especially if it means severing an intimate relationship. A frequent reaction to dealing with such trauma is to shut down emotionally, erecting a wall to block the pain. Still others feel a whirlwind of intense emotions which may include a sense of terror and helplessness, feelings of failure, and disdainful conflicting choices.

Perhaps it is so for you. Like Todd, your view of your life may seem ripped apart with a profound sense of rejection or loss. He put it this way, "For about one full year, I was in chronic emotional pain. Jan left me for someone else. If my spouse had died (as difficult as that would be), it would have been easier than divorce; because this was not only the loss of my wife, it was also the loss of her love for me. And I would have to see the *other man* frequently as I picked up my son who moved from home to home.

"I went to sleep at night feeling complete and ultimate rejection. I awakened in the morning, and within seconds of regaining consciousness, I felt the pain I fell asleep to. There was not a song on the radio I could listen to without feeling that emptiness. It was horrendous."

Some individuals feel such a shattered sense of self that they become overwhelmed with depression. Some go so far as to entertain thoughts of suicide. Marsha Means in her book, *Living with Your Husband's Secret Wars,* shares Veronica's story. Veronica's husband had an affair with a younger woman in their church. She just wanted to end the pain.

> I was so weary of the warfare, so tired of wondering what my husband would do. It was as if I heard a sweet voice saying, "Three to five minutes, three to five minutes, and it can all be over." That night I told my husband to go on to bed, that I was going to stay up for a while. I got a sharp knife and laid down in the bathtub, ready to take my life. Suddenly, I felt the overwhelming presence of the Lord. I could almost hear him whisper in my heart, "I am the source of your hope, even in your hopeless moments." And I couldn't do it. I had to choose life. But it's still incredibly hard. You know you can go forty days without food and three days without water, but you can't go five minutes without hope. (Marsha Means, *Living with Your Husband's Secret Wars,* Baker Publishing Group, Grand Rapids, MI, 1999, p. 28, used by permission.)

Take the Risk of Making Life Better

Hope comes when you embrace the pain and learn to value and trust your judgment. When you bear witness to your feelings, you make sense of your grief. As you walk through clouds of emotion and discard old, familiar ways, you come to terms with new, healthier ways of looking at and reacting to the everyday happenings of your life.

Jill, the runner, put it this way:

You have to leave your comfort zone...It's always going to be easier to do what's familiar— what you're used to. And even though that *familiar* may not be healthy, or get you to the finish line you're after, you do it because it's comfortable and you don't have to think about it or put in much effort.

Some time ago I went running with a friend. In our conversation after the run my friend said she was very careful about the shoes she wore so the cushion would protect her knees and back. I knew it was about time for me to get new shoes, but I hadn't wanted to spend the time to check mine out, or spend the money on new ones. That evening I took a good look at my shoes and was amazed what poor condition they were in. I had run a hole in the toe, and the outside of the heel was worn down. Also, the center tread of the ball was nearly worn through. I might as well have been running in my socks! But I was used to it. The feel of the run was *familiar.*

My daughter and I happened to be in the shopping mall a few days later. I stepped into the shoe store to check on the price of new running shoes. There was a terrific salesman there who set me up with the most cushiony shoes, and, being the only running shoes left in the store that were my size, I paid the price. That was a Saturday.

The following Monday, I was really excited about going out with my new shoes. I got up early and anxiously started my run. Those new shoes had air pockets in the heels. My feet and legs weren't used to having this extra bounce, let alone full tread. So I spent more time in the air than I did putting distance behind me. The shoes felt so different from what I was used to they threw me off balance. By the time I ran my three miles, I was hobbling.

The second day went the same way. I wanted to return the shoes and wear my old ones. Even though the new shoes, in the long run, would be healthier for me, I longed for the *familiar* feeling of being in control of where my feet were going! That day I threw the old ones in the garbage because I knew they presented too much temptation for me to return to my old ways.

Stick with it. Be willing to run the risk of being uncomfortable for awhile. *You have to make the good thing feel familiar before it can feel comfortable or right.* It took me a couple weeks, but I finally got control of my shoes!

Of course recovering from betrayal is a much bigger life change and takes more time than just breaking in a new pair of shoes. But the premise is the same. You've got to be willing to come out of your negative comfort zone and take the risk of making life better for yourself. Even little, focused modifications can direct you toward a safer, healthier, happier lifestyle.

You can't fight on the same terms as the betrayer because you'd never want to be so insensitive and ruthless. Your revenge, your way of fighting back, must be to reach outside your comfort zone, gain control of your life, and as Kami said, to "stand tall."

Avoid the temptation to say to yourself, "Why me? I can't do this. I give up." Don't question whether or not you can handle it. Instead, ask yourself, "*How* am I going to handle it?" Use your ingenuity and start looking for options and solutions to resolve your challenges. It is amazing how much more you can handle when you believe in yourself.

Rely on God

One woman, looking back, shared her feelings and advice about recovery. "Honestly, you have tremendous reserves you're not even aware of. I realized the truthfulness of that statement in the early years following my divorce. Through all the terrifying discoveries I experienced, I felt the Lord blessing me with growth, self assurance, tangible work and coping skills, knowledge, and extreme empathy. I even began to thank Him for the bad things that happened because I knew He was teaching me to put my priorities where they should be—to cultivate more tolerant and tender relationships with my family:

> I don't know where it came from, but I have this little saying that I've carried with me from one move to the next. "We are continually faced by great opportunities brilliantly disguised as insoluble problems."

> Take ownership of your challenges. Realize you are entitled to answers and directions from a loving God. I know He loves me, and I know He loves you. Have hope in your future, and move forward with a calm assurance that you are not alone.

With that assurance, talk to God specifically about what you need. Pray for His comforting influence, for strength, and for the ability to see things as they really are so you won't be deceived or view things out of proportion.

God knows all about your suffering. He truly loves you and wants you to feel happiness and joy. But His plan includes choices every individual is allowed to make. And sometimes individuals make choices that aren't really good for other people, or they affect others in an escalating adverse way, like dominoes falling one upon another. Everyone is blessed with adversity— opportunities for growth. God promises, however, to give peace to the faithful even in their sad times of trial, and to see them through those times if they'll obey and trust Him. Even if you can't see it now, as you obey God, trust that He will put you in places or situations in your life that will prove to help you in the future.

"God is our refuge and strength, a very present help in trouble. Therefore will not we fear, though the earth be removed, and though the mountains be carried into the midst of the sea; though the waters thereof roar and be troubled, though the mountains shake with the swelling thereof...Be still, and know that I am God" (Psalm 46: 1–3, 10).

God is in charge. He knows what we are thinking and feeling. He can soften the hurt and help us to see solutions. He can even prepare the path for the solutions to work.

Even if you're out of practice or have minimized your feelings for years, you can learn to listen to God's whisperings, to tune in to that still, small voice and know what is right for you now.

- First, give yourself permission to *feel* and time to think, ponder, and reflect.
- Write down your thoughts, feelings, and dreams. This action helps you not only vent, with no harm to others, but allows you to formulate short-term and long-term desires and goals. You may write your thoughts and experiences in a journal or diary. Or, if you are the creative type, it may benefit you to write poetry or stories.
- Foster an attitude of gratitude. Force yourself to look for and become aware of the good things in your life—the spring tulip that sprouts through the crevice in the rocks and produces a

magnificent red bloom, the unexpected shower of needed rain in the summer, the welcome call from a friend: "I was just thinking of you and thought I'd call to see how you're doing."

■ Learn to pray boldly, not with just words, but with your whole being. Ask God for inspiration that will bring you joy. Be specific. "I've done everything I can think of. I've got to have a job to provide for my family. Please help me find a door that will open. Please have someone call, or tell me who I should call, or where I should go."

■ Then listen, not necessarily with your ears. Listen with your *feelings*. Some have expressed answers from God as sympathetic vibrations in their hearts and minds.

■ Deliberate over what you *feel* you should do, and make a decision. Don't give this power to someone else. Stop waiting for others to tell you your choices are okay. Trust yourself. You can come up with the right answer.

"By affirming your opinions, ideas, and dreams," said Dr. Jane Greer, "you bring your internal messages to the surface and begin to reestablish trust in your own judgment. And as you become more self-reliant, you foster the emotional independence necessary for ending gridlock." (Jane Greer, *Gridlock,* Doubleday, p. 167, used by permission.)

■ Ask God again if the direction you *feel* you should go is right.

■ Listen. If you *feel* uneasy or confused, go back and pray again and follow this process from that point. If your decision is right, you will *feel* peace and calm, coupled with a drive to move forward.

■ Take appropriate action based on your *feelings*. "Take time to deliberate; but when the time for

74

action arrives," said Andrew Jackson, "stop thinking and go in."

- Now give yourself license to sense the miracles, for they will surely come. "There are only two ways to live your life," said Albert Einstein. "One is as though nothing is a miracle. The other is as though everything is a miracle."

- The more you listen to His voice and act upon what you're told to do, the more direction you will receive, and the more you will feel the reward of promised joy.

This is not to say that every choice you make will prove to be the absolute *right* answer for you. There will be times when you won't have all the information to formulate a good choice. There will be other times it won't appear *right* at the onset but will become obvious later that you made the *right* move. Each time you make a small decision and take action on it, you gain self-awareness and the ability to choose more confidently and wisely the next time.

Trust What You Know to Be True

You can expect to feel on top of things one day and desperately overcome the next. It isn't like the grieving process comes once and then is gone. It's like a yo-yo. It comes back and smacks you in the face when you least expect it.

A part of the grieving process we bring upon ourselves. It's like a different kind of battering—the "what if I had..." and the "I wish it were..." It's the self-inflicted remorse, looking back and kicking ourselves because we couldn't make it all roses.

Enid had to constantly remind herself of what happened so she wouldn't lapse into melancholy or feeling sorry for herself. Like the day she packed clothes for her husband, who had turned himself in to the authorities. "She zipped up the bag and stood to take it downstairs to the front door. She dabbed at her eyes. She had been crying again. She chastised herself for that, too, but the trouble was, she usually didn't even realize she'd begun. It was strange, this mourning business..." (Benson, *Blind Trust* p. 266)

Allow yourself an appropriate period for grieving, but don't let it go on indefinitely. If you become uncontrollably depressed, or find that your grief prevents you from doing your job or interacting with your family, seek professional help.

Enid felt at times as if she'd fallen into another dimension, where she could talk and people didn't hear her, where she could walk and not make a sound. She began to question her own sanity; she began to question everyone's sanity. Not only had Joe been able to get away with his lies before he, quote, got caught, unquote, but it appeared to her he was able to do pretty well afterward as well. He had told her up was down and down was up and she had believed him; now he was telling others—the media, especially, and in due course the United States Attorneys and the grand jury—the same thing and, incredibly, he was making headway there too. Enid questioned the very existence of reality. She took nothing for granted. *I used to know 1 plus 1 is 2,* she thought, *now I'm not sure. Now I have to question where I learned that, and who taught me; now I'm thinking, hey, maybe 1 plus 1 is 97. Who's to say it isn't?* (Benson, *Blind Trust* p. 311)

Whenever you sense you're heading into a tailspin of self-doubt, get out your reality checklist again and remind yourself of what you know to be true. *Trust what you know to be true.* Accept where you are and make the conscious decision to move forward.

Here are a few additional actions you might consider to help clear your thinking and promote sound judgment in the process of moving forward:

■ Simplify your life

Trauma and grief naturally overwhelm your normal coping skills. Things you could generally handle before may feel like too much now. Slowly add duties and activities as you can handle them.

■ Pace yourself

When even the basics seem overwhelming, break the whole into pieces and tackle each piece independently, pacing out your tasks in a step-by-step fashion to complete the whole.

■ Be realistic in your expectations

Realize you are not in control of what others have done or choose to do. Take control of what is yours and leave the rest to the agency of others.

■ Read the scriptures daily

By reading the accounts of those people who fought on the Lord's side, you gain insight and strength to fight your own battles and to make wise choices.

■ Listen to music

Some individuals find music a great help in working through grief. Being selective about what you listen to can have a definite bearing on your attitude. Avoid music with lyrics about betrayal and sadness. Instead, select songs with messages that inspire and uplift you. Sometimes it's the actual words of a song;

sometimes it's the melody; sometimes it's the beautiful memories of when or how it was sung.

Music alone can put a smile on your face and make you feel cheerful and happy. Music can make you feel like facing your challenges with determination and accomplishing what needs to be done. It can invigorate you—make you feel strong, excited, awake, and alive. Music can create for you a reverent atmosphere as well. There is great power in music.

■ Exercise

Even with limited mobility, there is some form of exercise everyone can do, even if it is just working the eye muscles, or concentrating on specific finger or toe movements. One woman purchased a punch bag and used it frequently to release frustration.

■ Eat properly and get ample rest

When you're fed and rested, all situations seem more manageable. Eating proper food aids your body's effort to function at its highest capacity, helping you control your thoughts, actions, and reactions. High proteins, such as meats and dairy products, help the blood sugar remain stable so emotions are less likely to run uncontrollably high or low. Many people, when under stress, eat too much or too little, resulting in additional distress and discomfort. Eating small meals throughout the day contributes to stable body functions and a more steady state of mind.

Proper rest is absolutely crucial, and yet sometimes extremely difficult to attain. Studies show that in the absence of adequate restorative sleep, the mind can actually generate distortions and out-of-control thoughts that otherwise would not happen if the brain were allowed to rest. When going through any trauma, while it is important to face the issue, it is also important to take breaks from the drama. Rest is a critical break that allows your body and mind to rejuvenate.

■ Relax

Proper relaxation is also vital as it allows you to recall the full purpose of your existence, the gift of enjoying who you are, and the wonderful things you want to do in life. While recovering from betrayal, occasionally pamper yourself. Take bubble baths, use candlelight, take a drive, engage in appropriate shopping, meditate on life's incredible offerings, recall pleasant memories. Calm your nerves and reward yourself for your hard work and the good choices you've made.

■ Cry

One woman was asked how she coped with depression and the helplessness she felt. Her response: "I frequently cleanse myself in a baptism of tears!"

■ Remember the good times and be grateful

"One thing I did that helped," Sarah says, "is that I scanned through my photo albums, not long enough to look at him, but to see the smiles on all the faces, the good times we had. This reminded me that all was not in vain. My children did have a fairly good childhood and I experienced a lot of good times. Because of this, the time invested in the relationship was not a failure."

Don't let toxic emotions rob you of the good things in your life. Just as every cloud brings a silver lining, so too are the clouds of your life lined with the silver reflections of the love of family, the security of great friends, the tender feelings of good times past, and all of the better times to come.

Hopefully you are in good health. If so, be grateful. If not, be grateful you are where you are, because things could always be worse. As someone once said, "It is not the end of the world until it *is* the end of the world." If you have plenty of money, be grateful. If not, be grateful for what you do have.

Which good things will you treasure from the past? What priceless lessons have you learned that will help shape your tomorrows?

"Following the discovery of my husband's double life," says Sarah, "he remained in a state of denial, refusing to be held accountable for the underground world he created. And he couldn't seem to jump out of it to answer to any of the needs of the real world left behind. As a result, he didn't work or produce money, even though in the past we had been quite wealthy. Because of this, I lost my house and my car. Shortly after my husband left me, my mother was diagnosed with cancer and died. And my children all seemed to be emotionally spinning. But, I was grateful. I really was. I was grateful I had children. I was grateful for the many years I spent in that beautiful home. I was grateful that somehow I got out of that dangerous relationship without a life-threatening sexual disease. And I was grateful for the time I got to spend caring for my mother and all the wisdom she gave me. I kept thinking that if I have to go through this painful time, the least I can do is temper it with love, life, and laughter. I told people my husband may have *gotten me,* but he did not get *all* of me. Maybe this was, instinctively, my way of getting back at him. If he ever thought he could destroy me if I didn't go his way, he was wrong. So I took the small part of me he didn't get and rebuilt my life without him."

■ **Look ahead with hope instead of dwelling on the negatives of the past**

One individual remarked, "This year my husband and I went to San Diego to visit our son stationed at the Miramar Marine Base. During our visit, we took a short boat trip to fish in the ocean. The water was extremely rough that afternoon. The waves tossed the boat as I had never experienced. The seasoned fishermen on board told us to keep our eye on the shore or on something steady like the horizon, where the swelling water and sky met. They said that would prevent us from getting sick. For the most part it worked! And it reminded me of how our lives can remain relatively steady even with the barrage of obstacles we face when we stay focused on our righteous goals and our forward momentum."

■ Lean on the Lord

Do you know what it means to *lean on the Lord?* It means you accept His will for you. It means you trust that He will keep His promises to help you. It means you look to Him for answers and solutions. It means you praise and thank Him for the peace He sends and for His unconditional love and example. The problems ahead of you are never as strong as the power behind you when you lean on the Lord.

■ Never abandon faith and hope

Faith and hope provide you with the power and the will to do. One Bible dictionary tells us that faith is a principle of action and power. The possessor of true faith will always be moved to some kind of physical and mental action. Faith brings you the assurance of the fulfillment of the things you hope for. Let hope and faith give strength and peace beyond your tears.

One woman's favorite scripture is 2 Timothy 1:7. "When I suffered most," she said, "I printed this scripture on a poster and hung it on my refrigerator. 'For God hath not given us the spirit of fear; but of power, and of love, and of a sound mind.'"

Cling to the words *power, love,* and *a sound mind.* Focus on your forward movement, not the hurt from the past. Pray for help to give up the bitter feelings that frustrate your happiness. Lift up your heart and know you are never alone. Let the Lord comfort you. Lean on Him. Trust Him. Take action. Do all that is in your power. Then know that, in time, the Lord will send you help in one form or another.

"Peace I leave with you, my peace I give unto you: not as the world giveth, give I unto you. Let not your heart be troubled, neither let it be afraid" (John 14:26).

The third step—Action

Get on your knees and ask for God's blessings and direction; then stand on your feet and do what is right. Act—don't just react.

CHAPTER FOUR

The Fourth Step—Authorization

*A man who doesn't trust himself can never really
trust anyone else.*—Cardinal De Retz

Whether you choose to reconcile with the betrayer
or separate, certain issues may linger and cause you to
struggle over the weeks, months, and years ahead. Two
issues, in particular, might plague you: rebuilding trust
and forgiving. Forgiving will be covered in Chapter 5. This
chapter considers what it takes to reprogram and
authorize yourself to rebuild your life and experience trust
again—as Enid might say, "So you can be assured that
one plus one actually does and always will equal two!"

Betrayal trauma happens when a person or
institution you depend on for survival violates you in
some way. The manner in which that trauma is
processed and remembered is influenced by the degree
of trust and intimacy *you believed* existed between you
and the betrayer. The intensity of that experience, when
the betrayal is between intimate partners, can be painful
and take time to subside. Your chances of recovery,
achieving balance, gaining control, and feeling
enjoyment in your life are improved greatly when you
share your feelings associated with the betrayal.

Often betrayers demand silence because they do not want anyone to know about their unacceptable behavior. *Silence from the betrayed gives control to the betrayer.* And in some cases, the betrayed has given his or her life for that silence.

Aside from the betrayer's demand for silence, people in general have a tendency not to share with others what might be going wrong in their lives. Maybe it's a matter of pride or embarrassment. But sometimes it's because they feel private matters should be kept private. And in a healthy relationship, this isolation from the rest of the world is one of the most incredible aspects of the union between a husband and a wife.

When a caring partner accepts your inadequacies and is willing to discuss with you your most emotionally intimate thoughts and feelings, you can feel safe and secure. But in the case of betrayal, this isolation can be devastating, diminishing your objective vision and warping your perspective.

Even when there is reconciliation, you must exercise caution in bridging the respectful gap between what should remain private and what should be shared. Sharing may only be with your mother or a trusted friend, but authorize yourself—give yourself permission—to *talk to someone.* And remember, that person will not be much help to you if he or she only encourages you to forget about the incident(s), to try not to relive it, and just *get on with your life.* The person you choose to share your thoughts and feelings with must be someone capable of keeping a confidence. This person must be understanding, patient, a sympathetic listener, and someone who will allow you to talk about the traumatic event(s) over and over again.

One woman who witnessed and experienced the horrors of Nazi Germany and the invasion of Berlin— being raped, watching her family die, having her home bombed, and so forth—survived the war and later got a job with a businessman. The businessman insisted on two-hour lunches. He also insisted they eat quickly so the rest of their lunchtime could be spent walking together. During their walks, he asked her over and over to tell him about her experiences and her feelings, fears, and anxieties. She explained that having someone to talk to who was willing to listen to the same things over and over and over saved her sanity.

Find someone you can talk safely with to air your concerns, someone you could even yell at about your problem and not have him or her take it personally. Sometimes, just in the act of sharing your feelings with someone, you can experience an actual physical stress reduction. Often, in the process, you come up with your own solutions.

Dr. Richard L. Williams explains this process from the listener's point of view. "Many professional counselors incorporate a three-step process into their empathic listening skills to help their patients express strong feelings, and even emotions...The technique is called VVS: The first step is to let the person ventilate his or her thoughts and feelings. If, however, by ventilating the person actually becomes more agitated, back off from this technique. The second step is to validate the person with positive or reinforcing feedback. And the third step is to provide forms of support in ways you feel are appropriate such as saying, 'What can I do to help?'" (Richard L. Williams, *Coaching Strategies to Improve Performance*, Vision Publishing Company, Sandy, Utah, 1999, p. 33, used by permission.)

Talking with supportive people in a safe environment is one of the most effective ways to work through trauma or grief. Doing so will help you:
- Release pent-up emotions
- Gain a clearer perspective of what happened

- Recognize, weigh, and prioritize your options, so you don't move forward too impulsively
- Identify your needs and provide emotional strength and support
- Develop self-confidence

Share Your Experience With Family

When you find yourself a victim of betrayal, your family can be a refuge. Do you have a parent or a brother or sister who is willing to share a problem with you, to be a considerate, listening ear? This person should not be someone who undermines your comments and actions, or someone who punctures your confidence, but a parent or sibling who can help you unravel the confusing events you've experienced—one who can orient you—someone you trust to be a temporary anchor.

"I always enjoyed the fact that my husband and I were, for the most part, very private about the intimate details of our relationship," said Sarah.

A lot of what negatively happened within the marriage stayed within the marriage, and he reminded me of that often. A part of me now wonders if that was a part of his tactic—to keep me from talking for fear I might find out other people did not engage in some of the same practices he did, namely pornography.

When the marital problems became larger than the marriage commitment, I got to the point where I felt, in order to survive, I needed to break away from our privacy bond to get support. It was *so* hard to do. For months, I couldn't tell anyone what was wrong. At first, I told my sister-in-law that there were problems, but I couldn't get myself to admit what they were. Then, finally, one day I told her that Richard had a problem with pornography and had been going to strip joints for years, and Heaven only knew what else. I told her that he was also very defensive to my questions and had even accused me of possessing behaviors worse than his. Her reaction was such a reality check. She was appalled that Richard would do such a thing, and said she didn't know of anyone who did that, even worse, behind their spouse's back.

I was so shocked to hear that news that I called my brother, who was quite liberal on many matters, and told him what was going on. His response surprised me even more. It wasn't his liberal opinion on pornography and strip joints that shocked me, it was his admission that if he ever did engage is such behaviors, his wife would surely know about them.

I learned a whole new world of information that day, and in the days ahead, as my support group expanded and opened my eyes to a bigger world around me.

In the world of betrayal, when a man is the victim, he becomes especially vulnerable to anxiety, depression, and guilt. In general, men are expected to bear their struggles in private. This is partly because society can't seem to view outward emotional expression in the same package with masculinity. As a result, men are less likely to ask for or receive emotional support. But they must. And often the family is where they find it. For men and for women, telling trustworthy family members what's happening, asking questions, and getting feedback can be like welcome rain on parched soil.

"October 22nd came, and I had agreed to meet my wife at the paralegal's office to sign the divorce papers," said Todd.

SHATTERED

Of course, in total defeat I went. I signed, hatefully. I left, without saying a word. I went home and sat on the stairs in total loss, total defeat, total emptiness. I cried and cried and cried. I laid there drained, with nothing left. In a state of complete nothingness and sorrow, I just stared at the ceiling. At this moment, the phone rang. I dragged myself to the phone and answered.

"Hi Todd." It was my sister Lynn. She and I had always been very close. "How are you doing?" she asked. I could not believe her timing. Actually, I could. I needed so desperately to talk to someone I knew loved me. And Lynn always seemed to be in tune with where I was emotionally.

I told her my story. She asked if I would like to come to her home to get away from all of it, and spend the weekend in a couple weeks. Her husband, being a pilot, had access to buddy passes, and she sent me one. Three weeks later, when I flew to her home, I was wrapped in the arms of a caring and loving sister. We talked a lot. Her sweetness and love for me reminded me of the wonderful family I had. It brought me home. Her children were fun, kind, loving. Her husband, always the jokester, put a comical slant on the negatives in my life, implying my *rightness* and my former wife's *wrongness,* which was of course not true and all in jest.

Talking with and making a conscious effort to listen to those you *do* trust not only gives you a reality check, it provides renewed energy, courage, and a hope that your world can and will be safe again.

Martha had pretty much kept her troubles to herself. She lived in the Midwest. Most of her extended family lived in the East.

I don't know that I was necessarily embarrassed about my situation. I think I was just plain overwhelmed and hurt. I had a giant emotional bruise. I mean, I was in shock. Even though I proved his actions to be true, I couldn't believe my husband could be that deceitful, that cunning, that uncaring about me and the children.

By then, my husband and I were sleeping in separate rooms. I had hidden in a box the evidence I discovered—credit cards, loan papers, etc. And even though words weren't exchanged, I knew he knew that I had them. Night after night, when I went to bed, my husband dressed in dark clothes and stealthily went around in the darkness looking for that box. It was the scariest time of my life. I thought I was going to be strangled in my sleep.

I turned to God as I always did. I anchored my survival on Him. I told Him how terrified I was and that I desperately needed help. I couldn't see a light at the end of the tunnel, not even a flickering glimmer. I was thinking there was no hope and maybe I should just end it. But my brother called to see how I was doing. He sensed my hopelessness and somehow knew what I was thinking. He told me I couldn't do it, that I had to remember the children and live for them, and for getting them out of this mess. We talked for a long time.

Even with the craziness around me, I was able to sleep that night. To this day, I feel my brother's phone call saved my life. And to keep me steady, he further arranged for my cousin, my sister, and my parents to take turns calling me often to see me through.

Share Your Experience With Friends

Knowing that you belong to something much larger than yourself tends to make you feel less victimized, less prone to bitterness. When sadness crowds in, the society of good friends, like family, can be a valuable resource—people who believe in you and can help you believe in yourself.

Having been betrayed, your feelings are tender and you're vulnerable to the fear of being hurt again. This sometimes makes it difficult to reveal your secrets to others because you're afraid they will turn you away or make light of your problem. But remember, caring people care. Your true friends will not reject you. They will build a wall around you to buoy you up and fortify you.

If one person or another does not show the kind of care and concern you need, don't take his or her lack of support as a sign of personal rejection. Maybe this person is unable to relate to a problem of this magnitude, or maybe your friend is preoccupied with his or her own problem. Try again with other friends. Eventually you will find those who are willing and able to help.

Marla, a thirty-year-old businesswoman, recalls, "I remember when I found out my brother was gay. I was really distraught. I finally decided to call my mother-in-law, who I always considered one of my close friends, and a person I highly respected. Upon hearing my heartache, she seemed distant and uncaring. She said, 'I'm sorry to hear that, but I have to go. Someone is at the door.' And then it hit me. The degree of problems we had discussed before were nowhere near what I was currently sharing."

Roman author, orator, and politician, Cicero once said, "The shifts of fortune test the reliability of friends." Brainstorming with a reliable friend can help you pick out from an array of possible actions which option may benefit you the most. If you spend time with mentally healthy friends who are involved in healthy relationships, they will do what they can to reconfirm your basic belief in mankind. And if they have observed actions leading up to the betrayal, they can help you confirm the truth.

Enid's friend Ladonna felt it was her *job* to aid Enid in retaining her emotional stability. She realized "Enid not only needed damage control on many fronts, and that included the media, but she also needed a support system to help her get back up from Joe's bodyslams. She needed to realize that she wasn't less of a person because she'd been taken in by Joe...Each in their own way, they had all been hoodwinked, just as they had all unwittingly facilitated Joe's con. They had all dealt with Joe as honest people—thinking he was honest as well." (Benson, *Blind Trust*, pp. 281–82.)

Consider this simple parable. You run your right hand down a wooden railing, and in the process— ouch!— a painful sliver becomes embedded in the palm of your hand. Being right-handed, you'll find it nearly impossible to handle the tweezers accurately enough with your left hand to remove that little piece of wood. If the sliver is left there, it might fester and become a bigger problem requiring professional attention. But if you hand the tweezers to a competent friend, often his or her view and coordination facilitates the sliver's removal, and instantly relieves the pain.

Another thing to remember is that a friend can administer one of life's choicest medications— companionship in laughter. This may sound odd to include laughter at such a traumatizing time as dealing with betrayal. However, a good laugh can bring you out of a frustrated mood and be so powerful that you feel a natural high afterward. Some hospitals even use laughter for patient therapy. Recent research suggests your body chemistry changes when you laugh, which could affect your immune system and the healing process.

In the last twenty-four hours have you had a good laugh? Are you aware of the power and energy that comes with laughter? It is good exercise and helps you cope with anger and fear. Like a giant bandage, laughter prevents boredom, reduces conflict, and eases feelings of isolation and loneliness. When you laugh with a friend, all things seem more manageable. This quote exemplifies the power of laughter: "Those who laugh, last!" (anonymous)

Why not meet a friend for dinner tonight? Say, "I have a serious problem. I know it's my problem, but I need your help..." After your visit, express your gratitude profusely for his or her listening ear and the wondrous gift of friendship.

It's easy enough to find plenty of friends
When life's gliding smoothly along,
But give me the one who's a friend in real need
When everything seems to go wrong.

When fortune's against us and clouds hide the sun,
That's the time when we're needing the cheer.
Oh, give me the true friend who's ready to help
At the hour when life's sad and drear.

It's easy enough just to smile with the gay,
And join in the laughter and glee.
But one who stands ready in sickness and trial
Is the one who's a real friend to me.
(Ida Romney Alldredge, "A Friend Worth While,"
1924, used by kind permission of the author's
family)

Write Your Experiences in a Journal

Along with your reality checklist, consider keeping a journal or dated record of what occurs and how you feel, so you can track patterns of behavior and events. Over time, keeping a journal not only helps you discern fact from opinion (which you can rely on when discussing your feelings with others), it allows you to get in touch with (and sometimes let go of) your feelings about the betrayal.

Terra Wellington, a consumer wellness expert, said, "Journals or diaries are places where you can offer up the words of your soul for no one's consumption but your own and, instead, provide inner healing and reflective joy...Along with the proper therapeutic care, journaling can help people reconnect with their feelings after deep loss, severe stress, or emotional distress...Besides goal setting, journal writing can heal physically, emotionally, and mentally." (Terra Wellington, "Free Your Spirit with the Written Word," *Balanced Living Column,* http://www.terra wellington.com/Column2004/082004.htm [Feb. 18, 2005].)

Look to Others for Support

Another beneficial resource available to you is support groups, whether they are in the form of meetings held at local facilities or on the Internet. One study, conducted by University of California professor, Dr. Morton Lieberman, showed the effectiveness of online supportive help for women with breast cancer. The results were impressive—a significant decrease in depression, an increased zest for life and hope for the future, and a deepened spirituality. This study also showed a significant decrease in the patient's negative reactions to pain. (Morton A. Lieberman, et al,

"Electronic support groups for breast carcinoma: A clinical trial of effectiveness" *Cancer,* Feb. 3, 2003, pp. 920–925.)

Studies have also shown that Type A middle-aged males *with few friends* were three times more likely to die (69% vs. 17%) than Type A middle-aged men *with friends* (Kristina Orth-Gomer and Anne Birgitte Unden, "Type A behavior, social support and coronary risk: Interaction and significance for mortality in cardiac patients," *Psychosomatic Medicine*, Vol. 52, 1990, pp. 59–72.)

Participating in support groups tends to broaden your thinking. Support groups can be extremely effective in helping you realize that others have gone through similar troubles and have not only survived but are living healthy, happy lives. Support groups can provide many benefits:

- They can show you that you are not alone in what you are going through.
- They give you the opportunity to learn new ideas about how to cope by hearing other people's experiences.
- They offer a time for some relief from your pain.
- They afford a chance to gain new friendships.
- They provide an opportunity to reduce guilt by talking with people who have dealt with the same situation in a similar fashion.

By participating in support groups you can not only *receive* help, but *offer* help, fulfilling a yearning for the soul: to know that you are still a valuable human being with credible thoughts and feelings that can benefit others.

Online support groups can be found easily on your computer. For example, on the search engine Google, in the search space, type the words "betrayal support group." This will lead you to a number of support group possibilities.

As you seek support, whether it is for the purpose of venting your frustrations or of asking and receiving directions on how to get out of your box, and whether you are choosing to confide in a family member, a friend, an online community of friends, your ecclesiastical leader, or a professional counselor or therapist, be aware that their support is based on the information they have at hand. Unless they are personally involved, as the situation might be with a family member or friend, they can only respond to the input *you* provide. How you present your experience will make a tremendous difference in the reaction and type of support you receive.

It is critical that you present the facts without embellishment, and clearly label all other information as your opinion or assumption. Don't shove your needs to the back burner or expect others to know intuitively what they are. Recognize and acknowledge what you need. Then clearly state what you are asking for.

As you receive feedback from your supporters, remember you don't have to agree with them. Talking things over with others helps you see your situation with more clarity. But, in the end, only you can determine what is right for you, regardless of the opinions of others.

Kami depended on many to see her through her ordeal. When asked how she managed after separating from her husband, she replied, "I worked with the law, and I started seeing a therapist to gain self-confidence. I surrounded myself with friends and family—mentally strong people—sort of as a security blanket. I prayed every day for things to work out."

Working with the law and with therapy helped, even though, in her instance, the abuse continued.

When asked how she finally got her former husband to stop harassing her, Kami replied:

That was the tough part. He was very slick and keen regarding the police. He would call and harass me at work to the point where he got me fired from my night job, and tried desperately to get me fired from my day job of 15 years. He called and called and called, nonstop. Then he showed up at my job, hid around corners, etc. I called the police so many times they found it a burden to keep coming to write up reports! I took up karate as a precautionary self-defense measure. And I tried to make sure I was never alone.

See the support she continued to look for? Family, friends, police, therapists, self-defense course. Calling in even more support to keep from losing her day job—eventually it all paid off.

I pulled my supervisor aside and told her what was going on. Once I did that, she was much more understanding. It suddenly all made sense. I was no longer looked on as someone who was slacking off and doing poor work. I was seen as someone who had a lot of strength, trying to do my work, raise my children, and yet was going through all this *stuff.* I was offered whatever time I needed to take care of everything. My former husband's picture was even posted with the lobby security to prevent him from coming into the building. And my co-workers offered to walk me to and from the train stations.

It was the best thing telling my supervisor. At first I was scared of being fired. I figured they didn't need this nonsense at work. But it was the opposite. They sympathized with me and offered to help me in any way possible. And because of their support, my former husband couldn't use my job as a means of intimidating me.

Also, as it turned out, my workplace offered me many resources I did not know were available. They introduced me to a program called "Lifeworks." It is a counseling/referral/legal/ medical/social-working program. The employee talks to them on the phone and they pull every resource available to help you, in all aspects. And it was all free to me! They also referred me to one of their other offices that had a special CIA-type team. They gave me pointers and tips on dealing with people like my former husband.

With all of this support, in time, Kami learned what she needed to do to rid herself of her abuser. She recalls some of the pointers given by this special team:

I was told that my former husband would probably try to contact me, cry, and make me feel sorry for him. This is a pattern often followed because individuals like that prey on your kindness and weakness. They warned me to get copies of the order of protection to the schools, since he tried to take my children once before. I was to inform the children that if he showed up for anything, they were to run and scream and call the police so he couldn't say, "Hey, it's okay. Your mom and I are fine now. She asked me to pick you up."

I was also warned that he would try to find me alone—on the staircase where I live, on my block, etc.—so I had to put my head on a swivel and always be aware and cautious. I was not to be intimidated by his threats with work and such because most likely he would not follow through with them. I was told my former husband was just using these tactics to force me to meet with him.

All of these proved to be true. He tried them all. He tried the desperate tactic of crying and begging. I was prepared, so it did not work. He tried the cocky attitude, "If you don't give in I'll..." I was prepared, so it did not work. He then tried the nasty approach, threatening to get me fired, cause trouble in my life, etc. I was prepared, so it did not work.

He ran out of things to try, but was persistent. I'll give him that. As long as I surrounded myself with friends and family until I was strong enough on my own, he was limited in how far he could go.

Develop Faith in God

Like Kami, much of your personal power is temporarily lost when you give more to the relationship than anyone should expect. One of the reasons this step in the process of recovery is referred to as authorization is because you must give yourself authority or permission to create your own autonomy, your own individual strength—a license to govern yourself and trust yourself.

In 1942, Alcoholics Anonymous, one of the first addiction-related support groups, began to recognize the importance of each person finding within himself or herself the strength to triumph over addictive behaviors or destructive thought patterns. Printing the following on small cards, they distributed them with the hope that their members would find the strength to overcome. Titled "The Serenity Prayer," the words are as follows:

God grant me the serenity to accept the things
I cannot change;

Courage to change the things I can,
And wisdom to know the difference.

Most people are familiar with the first three lines of this prayer, but they are not familiar with the rest of the prayer, which offers even more strength:
... And wisdom to know the difference.
Living one day at a time;
Enjoying one moment at a time;
Accepting hardships as the pathway to peace;
Taking, as He did, this sinful world
As it is, not as I would have it:
Trusting that He will make all things
Right if I surrender to His Will;
That I may be reasonably happy in this life
And supremely happy with Him forever in the
next. Amen (anonymous)

Relief can be felt when you understand that you do not have to be in *total* control of your life, that a loving God is in charge, and that, if you submit yourself to Him, He will direct your path. But you have to believe He will do this for you, that He and His promises are *real*. Developing a faith that allows you to draw from God's well of living waters helps the small picture of daily living fit into the big picture of what life is really all about. This belief, this fact, gives reason to your moments of greatest triumph or deepest despair. It helps alleviate the pain because it dispels the idea that you are being randomly picked on. However, *you* must do what it takes to *find Him*. How do you do that? You talk to Him, pour out your heart to Him. Read about Him in the scriptures. Talk to your friends about Him. Attend church. Whatever it is and whatever it takes, find within yourself your religious belief system.

One of the interesting things about believing in God, or developing the faith that there is a kind God who loves you, is that hope is always returned with that belief and faith. In other words, the more faith you offer, the more hope you receive.

For example, if you were going to have surgery tomorrow, you would have to have faith that your doctor was competent. There would be no way to really be sure your doctor was competent because you have not followed him around enough to really know. But he said he was, and you accept this by faith. Having faith in your doctor gives you the hope that your surgery will be successful. If you did not trust your doctor or did not have faith in him, you would most likely panic and believe your surgery would not go well.

Belief in God works the same way. The more you trust that God is real and is watching over you, the more hope you have that life, with all of its ups and downs, has a purpose and will ultimately go well.

Even the United States coins are imprinted with the words, "In God we trust," to remind everyone that they can't, or shouldn't, live their lives without Him. One passage in the Bible is particularly noteworthy in this regard: "Trust in the Lord with all thine heart; and lean not unto thine own understanding. In all thy ways acknowledge him and he shall direct thy paths." (Proverbs 3:5–6)

Trust and Care for Yourself

Developing faith in God strengthens belief in self and a belief that your life matters and that He has a plan for you. In this sense, faith provides a spiritual reservoir of support that can fuel your determination to succeed.

When you value yourself, it is easier to set reasonable expectations and limits on how to treat yourself and what you will and won't *allow* to happen to you.

You were born with yourself, and you will live with yourself each day until the day you die! *You are your primary responsibility.* Be loyal to yourself first—not in a selfish way but in a respectful way. Often you have given too much consideration to the other person and not enough to yourself. You must become your own best caretaker. When you practice good self-care, your mannerisms, words, and actions reflect an invisible aura or quality that automatically makes you less vulnerable. You are less likely to be targeted by those who take advantage of others. Give yourself approval to take care of yourself. "After all," said one therapist to his patient, "you are the best self you've got!"

Making a conscious choice to live a happy life (and making that choice may be a daily battle) means taking responsibility for yourself and overcoming the limitations imposed by the betrayal. Begin by asking yourself, "What are my greatest strengths? What are my weaknesses?" This is not a time for personal bashing but for taking a realistic look at yourself for the purpose of improvement—to help you have a positive yet realistic view of yourself. If you have difficulty identifying your strengths, ask one of your supporters to help you.

My greatest strengths are:

_____

_____

_____

_____

_____

_____

_____

_____

_____

My weaknesses are:

_____

_____

_____

_____

_____

_____

_____

_____

With some focus and effort, many of your weaknesses can be diminished, sometimes even turned into strengths. For now, recognize, develop, and work confidently with your strengths to move forward. When you are able to acknowledge your strengths, you feel secure and confident with yourself and less dependent on the betrayer's approval. Your self-esteem (how you measure your worth) does not depend on him or her or anyone else.

Self-confident people develop the belief that, within reasonable limits, they can and will accomplish what they hope, plan, or expect to accomplish. Those with healthy attitudes have realistic expectations. Even when things don't turn out as planned, they still maintain a positive outlook. People who are unhealthy in their attitude toward themselves rely on the approval of others to make themselves feel good.

This anonymous quote proclaims the power of attitude:

> The longer I live the more I realize the impact of attitude on life. Attitude, to me, is more important than facts. It is more important than the past, education, money, than circumstances, than failures, than successes, than what other people say or think or do. It is more important than appearance, giftedness or skill. It will make or break a company...a home...a church...a marriage. The remarkable thing is that we have a choice every day regarding the attitude we embrace for that day. We cannot change our past, we cannot change the fact that people will act in a certain way and we cannot change the inevitable. The only thing we can do is play on the only string we have and that is our attitude. I am convinced that life is 10% what happens to me and 90% how I react to it. And so it is with all of us, we are each in charge of our own attitude.

The way you perceive or interpret a situation affects your attitude dramatically. And your attitude affects what you say to others and to yourself. This also works in reverse. What you say to yourself influences how you perceive what happens to you. So be aware and in charge of what you say to yourself. Encourage yourself to get where you want to go by substituting positive, supportive, internal dialogue for unnecessary negative thoughts.

Are you putting yourself down without even realizing it? Are you undermining your own self-confidence? Pay attention to your internal voice. Is it working for or against you? To strengthen your internal dialogue, avoid the following:

■ Seeing life from an all-or-nothing viewpoint

You may be tempted to tell yourself, "When my behavior is not perfect, I am a total failure," instead of, "Everyone makes mistakes. I sometimes do, too." All-or-nothing thinking leaves you no room for flexibility or compromise. In your mind, if you give yourself no room for error, your focus turns only on what failed to work, rather than on what you did right and did accomplish.

■ Magnifying the negative/minimizing the positive

Don't think, "I am so stupid," or, "I'm really not as smart as everyone thinks I am." Instead, tell yourself, "Sometimes I do some pretty dumb things, but most of the time I come up with reasonably good ideas for the problems that arise." Life is so much easier to face when you bring forward in your mind the positives. Give yourself credit for trying, and trust your ability to do.

■ Discounting compliments

If someone gives you a compliment, don't tell yourself, "That person doesn't really mean that—they're just saying that because they feel sorry for me." Try telling yourself, "It's sure nice to know people appreciate me." Be honest with yourself. Accept the reality of a good thing!

■ Taking things too personally

Saying, "I didn't know they thought I was that horrible of a person," is being very hard on yourself. Tell yourself instead, "Suggesting I use less expensive goblets at our next Thanksgiving dinner is not a reflection of how stupid they think I am, but a suggestion on how to avoid having my expensive goblets broken." Although experience with your betrayer has led you to believe otherwise, the majority of people say things to express good things to you, not to confuse, demean, or belittle. Step out of the picture. Remove the reference to yourself as a personal target and then see how you understand the statement. If you still question the intent, ask for clarification from the person who made the comment. Gain enough facts to understand the true intent.

■ Accepting your emotions as truth

Do not think, "Because I feel afraid, I must really be afraid." Try thinking, "My emotions must be misfiring right now and making me feel afraid because this emotional reaction is not realistic to the situation I am facing." Consciously calm yourself. What do you see or what have you heard that has made you *feel* uncomfortable? Does it really merit fear?

■ Getting caught up in the guilt of *should* statements

If you concentrate on the guilt, you will find yourself saying, "I should have done more for that person and now they probably won't like me." If you are more reasonable with yourself, you will likely say, "I probably could have done more, but whatever I did was as much as I could do and, as my friend, he or she should know that." Within reason, verbalize your feelings. However, it may be your own expectations of self, not your friend's, that is producing the feeling of guilt.

The voice within you has a strong influence on you, so analyze your internal voice and make sure it treats you kindly, or do whatever it takes to adjust your voice to a more upbeat, positive tone. Shoot down all negative self-dialogue. Accept yourself for who you are and compliment yourself for your willingness to grow and learn. Grant yourself credit for everything you try, no matter how big or small the effort. Build a foundation of strength by using your good choices, experiences, and knowledge. Be patient with yourself. Give yourself a break for mistakes you have made as you learn to walk again, after being emotionally wheelchair-bound. Authorize do-overs! Your focus is to sculpt a new you and this may take time.

You *will* survive this betrayal even if the relationship does not. At some point, you will be able to overcome your fears with a newly constructed self-confidence and realize that not all people betray. You will know the red flags to look for and be willing to take risks. In doing so, you will be able to expand your life to new horizons and experience all the good things life has in store for you. Recovering from betrayal is hard work at times, but remember, you have better tools to work with now. As you build or rebuild trust and a belief in yourself, you will find it easier to feel hopeful and will be able to open the door to trusting others.

Seek Professional Help When Necessary

Often, victims of *betrayal trauma* suffer from Post Traumatic Stress Disorder or PTSD. This disorder is experienced also by war veterans, rape victims, and others participating in or witnessing life-threatening or highly traumatic events. According to the National Center for Post Traumatic Stress Disorder (NCPTSD):

People who suffer from PTSD often relive the experience through nightmares and flashbacks, have difficulty sleeping, and feel detached or estranged, and these symptoms can be severe enough and last long enough to significantly impair the person's daily life.

Most people who are exposed to a traumatic, stressful event experience some of the symptoms of PTSD in the days and weeks following exposure. Available data suggest that about 8% of men and 20% of women go on to develop PTSD, and roughly 30% of these individuals develop a chronic form that persists throughout their lifetimes.

An estimated 7.8 percent of Americans will experience PTSD at some point in their lives, with women (10.4%) twice as likely as men (5%) to develop PTSD. About 3.6 percent of U.S. adults aged 18 to 54 (5.2 million people) have PTSD during the course of a given year. This represents a small portion of those who have experienced at least one traumatic event; 60.7% of men and 51.2% of women reported at least one traumatic event. The traumatic events most often associated with PTSD for men are rape, combat exposure, childhood neglect, and childhood physical abuse. The most traumatic events for women are rape, sexual molestation, physical attack, being threatened with a weapon, and childhood physical abuse." (Department of Veterans Affairs National Center for PTSD, "What Is Posttraumatic Stress Disorder?" www.ncptsd.va.gov/facts/general/ fs_what_is_ptsd.html, [Feb. 22, 2005].)

The NCPTSD lists factors contributing to an individual's vulnerability. All of these factors will increase the seriousness of the trauma:

- Greater stressor magnitude and intensity, unpredictability, uncontrollability
- Sexual (as opposed to nonsexual) victimization
- Real or perceived responsibility
- Betrayal
- Greater perceived threat or danger, suffering, upset, terror, and fear (ibid.)

"PTSD is treated by a variety of forms of psychotherapy and drug therapy," says the NCPTSD. "There is no definitive treatment, and no cure, but some treatments appear to be quite promising, especially cognitive-behavioral therapy, group therapy, and exposure therapy. Exposure therapy involves having the patient repeatedly relive the frightening experience under controlled conditions to help him or her work through the trauma. Studies have also shown that medications help ease associated symptoms of depression and anxiety and help with sleep." (ibid.)

If you feel unable to cope with the aftermath of your betrayal experience, do not feel timid or ashamed to enlist help from a professional therapist or counselor, skilled with the proper knowledge and tools. This too may be a matter of benevolent self-care.

Rebuild Your Trust in Mankind

In the course of recovery, trigger points will arise that will force you to experience some of the feelings you had while you were being victimized. As you become aware of these trigger points and what has caused them, you can attain a more normal life. However, the effects of the original trauma must be respected, not only by you, but by those around you, to help you more productively move through the process of rebuilding trust in mankind.

Depending on the severity of the betrayal, you initially may not be willing to trust others for fear of being hurt again. And because of this fear, you might find it easier to assume that all people are like the betrayer. Following her betrayal experience, Martha felt all men were deceitful and cunning. She said, "I even wondered if men encouraged a belief in God just to keep women fearful and restrained. I questioned the integrity of every male I knew. As the weeks passed following my divorce, I began to think of my brother and my father and how they had never betrayed me, never been disloyal to me, never lied to me. I thought about my belief in God, and recounted the many times I'd experienced direct answers to my prayers. And slowly, inch by inch, I managed to see that there were honest men out there, that not all men were like my former husband. And I began to rebuild trust in others."

Some people do betray, and for reasons known or unknown, you found yourself the victim of one. But your freshly acquired awareness and new, emotionally lifesaving skills will help you avoid betrayal in the future.

As you authorize yourself to be in charge of self, explore trusting others. Remember, not all people are like your betrayer. Life does have its risks, but someone else's wrong choices shouldn't invalidate who you are and what you represent. When dealing with others, move cautiously, ask more questions, and look for behaviors that merit trust:

- Emotional attachment
- Consistent support with heart, ears, mouth, body, and time
- A genuine consideration and show of respect for your feelings, rights, and limits

Barbara, whose husband was guilty of repeated indiscretions, experienced the pain of betrayal and survived. No, she didn't just survive—she excelled! "Every princess dreams of growing up, marrying her prince, and living happily ever after," she explains.

Well, I wasn't any different. But *happily ever after* didn't happen for me. Bill betrayed me time and time again, one affair after the other.

During those rough years, I was fortunate to see the dead-end road that bitterness leads to. I recall a middle-aged, ailing woman named Grace, who lived in our neighborhood and needed some assistance with her yard, housekeeping, and doctor visits. I agreed to help. Many hours were spent with Grace. As the relationship grew, so did her willingness to talk about her past life. Soon, what began as a trickle surged into a billowing flood of hate, anger, and bitterness as she shared her feelings about what her former husband had *done to her. Hmmm,* I innocently thought. *It's not what he did to you that poisoned your life and heart, but what you have chosen to do to yourself.* Truly, Grace was a woman driven by bitterness and hate. It consumed her health, her hopes, and her ability to form and keep friendships. She had lost more than she ever should have in response to a husband's betrayal. A more vivid lesson could not have been designed to teach me this principle: *Avoid bitterness at all costs, or you will end up the greater loser!*

Facing the prospects of putting together the pieces of a shattered life can be overwhelming without the knowledge that we are prepared to conquer whatever lies before us. My divorce left me feeling like an unwanted hurricane had raged through my heart and life and had dealt nothing but loss and destruction as far as the eye could see. Surveying the damage can be paralyzing emotionally and physically if one focuses on what is lost. I chose to focus on what I still had—my four beautiful children, my faith, my talents, and my inborn drive to rise to meet the challenge. Whatever was ahead I knew I could overcome because I believed in myself and in my ability to consciously move forward to better days. The same gift of agency was given to each member of the human race, and I was going to use mine to overcome my present loss. I felt determined to make lemonade out of those bushels of unwanted lemons dropped on my doorstep. This season of sorrow came uninvited, but I would turn it into a season of strength and courage.

Fifteen years have passed now since my divorce, yet the lessons are fresh in my mind and continue to shape my life each day. When we do not understand why something happens in our lives or what we are supposed to learn from it, it can be unnerving. Peace can seem far out of reach. Having been betrayed by the one closest to my heart, my husband, made it initially hard for me to trust anyone. I focused on two things: trust in the Lord, and confidence in myself. By trusting in the Lord and my life-long relationship with Him, I was able to rely on my own feelings of self-belief and on my ability to make good decisions. Every day and every hour became a quiet walk with my Savior. Heartfelt prayers were my lifeline to peace. I leaned upon His strength to buoy me up as my own strengths increased daily.

My belief in the goodness of others helped me to be able to trust people again. At first a few, then others were added to my *safe circle*. Sharing the horrors of my shattered life with close friends helped lighten my burdens. Their sensitivity and respect for what my family had experienced assured me that I would again be fine, and even better than before.

Emily Dickinson stated, "We never know how good we are, until we are called upon to rise." Betrayal calls upon all that is innately good within us to rise...and rise we must...

The fourth step–Authorization

Give yourself permission to talk, to rebuild trust, and to act with confidence.

CHAPTER FIVE

The Fifth Step—Accountability

*It is not only for what we do that we are held
responsible, but also for what we do not do.*
—Jean Baptiste Poquelin Molière

Accountability represents the obligation each
individual has to justify or be responsible for his or her
words and actions. For example, if a person decides to
open a checking account, he or she will be given a check
register to account for every check written. This record
can show who each check was written to and for what
purpose. The amount of the check can be written and
subtracted from the account balance, resulting in an
ongoing financial history, showing how much money is
in the account. Some individuals choose to follow their
check history online instead of with the traditional
check register. Either approach, however, represents
accountability in the check-writing process.

Whether the individual decides to keep his or her
register current by tracking every check (or by
frequently viewing it online) is a matter of personal
choice. But if the individual chooses not to write down
check information or track the account balance, and a
check bounces due to insufficient funds, he or she cannot

rightly say, "It was the bank's fault," "Registers are just too complicated and time-consuming to keep up," "I'm too busy," or anything that seeks to justify irresponsible behavior. The fact is, he or she is accountable for the good or bad of that account and the consequences that follow.

Each individual on this earth has the right to choose—to know and make choices regarding good or evil—and to ultimately receive appropriate consequences for those choices. This is accountability in the process of life.

Own Your Part in the Betrayal

In the case of betrayal, both parties must claim some accountability—the betrayer for his or her inappropriate words or actions, and the betrayed for his or her reaction, most often, for not taking a firm stand against compromising behaviors. In fact, without the betrayed person, there is no betrayal.

Although it's true that there are times betrayed individuals are merely bystanders, rarely could they be considered completely innocent. More often than not, they have failed to do something, or have done something to contribute to the betrayal. That statement may be hard for you to accept, and rather than look at your error, you may find it easier and more comforting to point out the faults of the other person. But what good does that do? Does it change the fact that you were betrayed or move you out of the betrayer's reach? No. To safely move forward, you must take your head out of the sand and look at your actions or failure to act— in a sense, be accountable for your own checkbook register!

Did you use poor judgment staying in the relationship just because you didn't want to be alone?

Were you unwilling to stand up for yourself or leave because even though it was an abusive relationship, you were committed, it was familiar ground, or you knew what to expect? Did you allow your need for attachment to rule, causing you to tolerate repeated, abusive treatment? Did you feel you were unworthy of being treated with respect? Did you lose sight of who you are—a son or daughter of God—and fail to respect yourself?

"The fountain of content," said Samuel Johnson, an eighteenth-century essayist and poet, "must spring up in the mind, and he who hath so little knowledge of human nature as to seek happiness by changing anything but his own disposition, will waste his life in fruitless efforts and multiply the grief he proposes to remove." (Sophie Bevan, *The Gift of Inner Peace*, Ryland, Peters & Small, London, England, 2004, p. 8, used with permission.)

Take the obsessive searchlight off the other person and focus it on yourself and what is within your power to change. To diminish the chances of being victimized again, and to heal, you can and must take responsibility for your life—your thoughts, attitudes, and actions—and own your part in the betrayal. After all, you are the only person you can change anyway.

That said, it needs to be remembered that the betrayer will attempt to deceive you into believing you are responsible for more than your share. Classic maneuvers are to twist information to make it appear that you are the one with the problem; you are the one who made the mistake; you are the one being overly emotional and irrational; because of you, he or she had to....That's when you pull out your checklist and read it again so you remain in the real world and trust yourself, so you don't take responsibility for the fraudulent behavior of the betrayer.

As a person recovering from betrayal, you must be wary of attempts to blur the lines of accountability. Be true to yourself. Own your part, but allow the other person to be accountable for what he or she chooses to say and do. Those choices are independent from anything you could say or do.

Take Todd for example. Was he accountable for his wife's choice to give her affections to another? No. Regardless of what he did or did not do, she made that decision. He could not control her choices, only his own. He acted with integrity. Once she made the choice to leave him for someone else, Todd's accountability lay in how he dealt with her behavior and her choices. He could only be accountable for his efforts and actions, how he reacted, picked up his life, and moved on.

And what about Martha? "Yes," she said, "I'm aware I should have made a stronger stand years before. I don't feel absolved of that responsibility. But, that doesn't make me accountable for his choice to lie and steal. He owns that."

Many times, the irresponsible betrayer seeks out someone he or she perceives as vulnerable, as willing to take on more responsibility than what is actually required. Often this individual is someone who is *too* nice, he or she has a hard time saying no and can easily be taken advantage of. This trouble-free target loves life to the point he or she must ensure it runs smoothly. This person feels best when everyone is getting along, and when others seem to like him or her—relationships are smooth and pleasant. Sound familiar?

In proper balance, these are great attributes, and many individuals have them without being compromised by other people. However, a betrayer knows exactly how to use these attributes against you. He or she knows that, under pressure, you will buckle and head for the path of least resistance, hoping that as soon as possible, you will be back in your noncombatant comfort zone.

When a betrayer uses your good attributes against you, it is your responsibility to be alert, take a stand, and remind yourself, "I am a nice person, but I do not have to be so nice that I tolerate abuse or allow myself to do wrong things just to please other people."

For example, one woman loaned her credit card to her son because he was in a *real bind*—short of money and without a job. However, he was *looking* for work. Always wanting to be nice, for life to run smoothly, and for her son to like her, the mother agreed to loan him the credit card in case he needed gas on a trip he was making from Las Vegas to Los Angeles. When the son returned from Los Angeles and she discovered he had run up her card to its maximum, she was upset. Yet, fearful of confrontation and not wanting to cause more problems than already existed, she waited a few days to talk to him about the problem. She finally asked him, nicely, "What happened to my credit card? What are all these charges?"

He responded, "I can't believe you're upset. Why are you asking these questions? Don't you trust me? If you were a nice, Christian mother, and you really loved me, you'd pay these charges without making such a fuss! You know I've been in a bind. You've got plenty of money. I'll probably never have as much as you..."

How nice should a person be? Not this nice!

Taking responsibility for oneself, or being accountable for one's actions, includes the following:

- Realizing and accepting that you are responsible for every choice you make in life and for the consequences your choices create. No one else can be blamed for your poor judgment. No excuses can justify poor behavior.

- Knowing you, and only you, are responsible for your thoughts, attitudes, and actions.
- Accepting the fact that you are responsible for your spiritual, physical, and emotional health.
- Taking responsibility for how you react to others and how you see and talk to yourself.
- Being responsible for your emotions, talents, values, and intellect.

When a person fails to take responsibility for himself or herself, negative results such as the following usually happen:

- An undue dependence on others
- An underlying fear of oneself, others, and life
- The belief that one is a victim of life and its circumstances
- A feeling of chronic anger toward others, and life in general
- A lack of successful relationships
- A lack of trust
- A propensity for addictions
- An over-responsibility for the actions of others

Some of the words used to describe those who refuse to take responsibility for themselves are as follows: martyrs, users, blamers, stubborn, angry, depressed, selfish, irrational, out of control, and negative.

Develop Your Bill of Rights

Awareness is a choice. Acceptance, action, and authorization are all choices. The power to choose is yours. No matter what your circumstances, you have options and choices to make. Consciously choosing or not choosing, either way you make a choice. A person's agency is his or her supreme power here on earth. No other creature has this power. You are constantly exercising it, whether for your benefit or not. Just like the betrayer, you exercise your agency for good or for evil, and your conscience can always tell you the difference between the two. Defend your right of agency and respect the rights of others to exercise their agencies.

You have to live with the consequences of your choices. It is a given that you will make mistakes. It's not possible to make perfect choices all the time. But it is possible to consistently make better choices that you can live with and grow from when you respect and trust yourself, set reasonable limits, and have a clear idea of your identity as a son or daughter of God.

The more time you spend worrying about things you have no control over, the more powerless you feel. Do not surrender to the other person part of your power of choice. Take the risk of making life better for yourself. Consciously let go of what you are not responsible for and apply your energy to worrying, acting, and reacting to the things you do have control over. In that environment, you become a catalyst for change and you feel a sense of personal power and accountability about the choices you make. Remember the Serenity Prayer: "God grant me the serenity to accept the things I cannot change, courage to change the things I can, and wisdom to know the difference."

As Mahatma Gandhi said, "We must be the change we wish to see." Making that change, however, does not come about without plan or effort, and in the process, you might need to accept some new things about yourself. These new ideas or self-concepts can be formulated by creating a Bill of Rights for yourself. Keep in mind that these personal rights are based on respect for self, not selfishness. In other words, these rights do not infringe on the rights of others.

Think about yourself right now, respectfully, not selfishly. What is important to you? What rights are truly yours to have? Some areas to consider are:

■ Emotional

- ◆ You have the right to feel whatever you are feeling, regardless of what others may say, think, or feel about you.
- ◆ You have the right to maintain ties, socializing with family and friends.
- ◆ You have the right to express your feelings and verbalize your needs, confiding in whomever you choose to confide.
- ◆ You have the right to feel safe and secure and to seek support from others.
- ◆ You have the right to set personal limits and boundaries.
- ◆ You have the right, in a relationship, to be treated with respect in private settings as well as in public.
- ◆ You have the right to heal old, emotional wounds and, even with love, let go of a relationship with a betrayer.
- ◆ You have the right to trust your own judgment.

■ Financial

- ◆ You have the right to regard money the way you would like to regard money, regardless of what others may say, think, or feel about you.
- ◆ You have the right, in a relationship, to have a say in money decisions and to benefit from financial arrangements.

■ Physical

- ◆ You have the right to choose how you take care of yourself—what you eat, how you exercise, and

when and for how long you sleep.
- You have the right, in a relationship, to expect a fair distribution of work.
- You have the right, in a relationship, to expect non-violent, satisfying resolutions to conflict.
- You have the right to choose your friends and activities.
- You have the right to ask questions and check things out in your relationships.
- You have the right to walk away from a relationship when there is repeated abuse, to disengage from a relationship with a betrayer and no longer share intimate details of your day or overextend yourself.

■ Sexual
- You have the right to withhold sex and affection when you feel it is not safe or appropriate.

■ Intellectual
- You have the right to seek learning and education in the way you would like, regardless of what others may say, think, or feel about you.
- You have the right to your opinion whether or not other people understand or agree with you.
- You have the right to hold the other person accountable for inappropriate actions.
- You have the right to dream and set goals, and to work within personal limits to achieve them.
- You have the right to make a move that's critical to you without waiting for permission from someone else.
- You have the right to sense whether something is right or wrong, to seek more information, and then use what you know to make informed decisions.

■ Spiritual

♦ You have the right to believe whatever you would like to believe, regardless of what others may say, think, or feel about you.

♦ You have the right to obey God's laws and be empowered by them.

♦ You have the right to pray and receive inspiration to make righteous decisions and choices.

Are there items on the above list you need to be reminded of? Personalize your Bill of Rights by using the pronoun *I*, such as, "*I* have the right to choose my reaction in every situation." What is your Bill of Rights?

My personal Bill of Rights
Emotional—I have the right to:

Financial—I have the right to:

Physical—I have the right to:

_____

_____

_____

Sexual—I have the right to:

_____

_____

_____

_____

Intellectual—I have the right to:

_____

_____

_____

_____

Spiritual—I have the right to:

_____

_____

_____

_____

Hold Others Accountable

Few individuals begin relationships as abusers. But, as you already know, by the time the abuse or betrayal is identified, the person who was betrayed has invested a lot of time, energy, and hope in the relationship. He or she didn't get into the abusive situation overnight and won't get out of it that quickly either. This process of recovery requires much patience, courage, self-discipline, and commitment. Note how one thing leads to another in a downward spiral in connection with tolerating abusive treatment. But on the other hand, the spiral of good choices and accountability leads upward! As the betrayed, you deserve a pat on the back, or perhaps a standing ovation, for your efforts to heal and move forward with your life.

You have taken ownership of your part in the betrayal. You have chosen to react to your circumstances on the basis of your values, not on the basis of your emotions, nor on what (in the past) you simply accepted of yourself. You pray for discernment to see things as they really are and to understand the difference between right and wrong, and you deliberately choose to follow your compass of personal integrity. You realize nothing is as powerful as personal choice, and just as you must be accountable for your thoughts, actions, and feelings, so must others.

Because of your nature and your habit, it might take some practice to relinquish ownership of some of the actions of the other person, and to hold the other person accountable for getting himself or herself wherever he or she needs to go. But remember, just like you, the other person has agency to decide his or her priorities and the right to receive an appropriate reward or consequence for his or her actions.

If you haven't already, you will move through an emotional separation. For some individuals this will be more painful than for others. This type of change involves a feeling of loss which will include a certain amount of anxiety, loneliness, awkwardness, and sadness. Be sensitive to yourself. Share your feelings with someone you trust, and remind yourself that those feelings are natural but temporary as you work through the separation process.

Depending on your previous reliance on the betrayer, you may find it difficult to use caution with open dialogue. You may still have hope that the other person will be reasonable. However, more often than not, as before, the betrayer will use any information you provide to manipulate you, your environment, and the happenings of your day. Be watchful.

Many of the problems that come with letting go and allowing others to be responsible for themselves are resolved by taking responsibility for yourself and remembering what you stand for, as discussed in Chapter 3. When an occasion arises where an individual asks something of you, stop and consider, "Does this person's request agree with my value system or Bill of Rights?" If yes, then you are not compromising yourself by fulfilling the person's request but actually helping that person.

If the request does compromise your value system or Bill of Rights, stop, and instead of accepting the responsibility, try to help the other person understand why you must not do it. Consider offering solution ideas that might help the other person be responsible and fulfill the request alone. If this person chooses to demean you or to demand your cooperation, step back and protect your *emotional self.* Again calmly refuse to accept the request. This type of behavior on the part of the other person signals his or her lack or unwillingness to be responsible for self. Yet, more importantly, the irresponsible person's words and actions say more about how he or she really feels about you. That person is willing to *use* you. Is that the type of person you want to be socially, emotionally, mentally, or physically intimate with? Hardly!

To further demonstrate this point, consider purposely watching the other person and choosing to hold him or her responsible to the same degree you are now willing to hold yourself responsible. Reverse the previously given list and now place all those points onto the other person. How well does he or she hold up to the test of being accountable? Is this person willing to be responsible for the following:

- How he or she decides to manage life?
- Not blaming others for choices made?
- Not making excuses to justify behavior?
- All of his or her thoughts, attitudes, and actions?
- His or her spiritual, physical, and emotional health?
- How he or she reacts to others?
- How he or she sees and talks to himself or herself?
- All of his or her emotions, talents, values, and intellect?

The same words listed before are also used to describe this type of person: martyr, user, blamer, stubborn, angry, depressed, selfish, irrational, out of control, and negative.

Do you see how this works? Remember, your responsibility is first to yourself, and then to influence for good the lives of those around you. It is not your responsibility to *fix* others, or to live their lives for them, or to pick up the pieces, or to fill in the gaps for those things that are their responsibility first.

Kami feels strongly about being responsible:

In time, I heard my husband stole from others. He pulled several scams that caused him to be wanted by the police in different states. So he fled. Because he had access and everything was in my name only—the house, credit cards, etc.— he left me carrying the burden of thousands of dollars of debt. I could have thrown in the towel and given up, but I chose to stand tall, handle my responsibilities, and do what I had to do for me and my children.

Mind you, I don't hate him. I feel sorry for him. I believe I was given one of the toughest tests yet. And I feel I passed that test! I also feel that because I stood for what was right, somehow, some way I helped him, even if in just a little way, and I became a stronger person out of it all. I stopped blaming myself for his actions. I knew that no one deserved to be treated the way he was treating me. I tried with everything I had to help him understand what he was doing. You know, there might be times when individuals like that can be helped, but not when your life is at risk!

While no one is perfect, healthy relationships come about when two people remain aware of who they are and their accountability to themselves first and to the other person second. Each behaves in an acknowledging, accepting way toward himself or herself. Each has standards and limits or boundaries that are clearly respected by the other. There is stability within the relationship because of consistent, considerate behavior, where each one follows through on what he or she promises to do. When human error or lapses in responsibility take place, the parties recognize the mistakes and they adjust accordingly. There is a desire to prevent either party from being hurt. An equality exists in the relationship, a genuine interest in the other person's well-being, and a desire to ensure that his or her good mental health remains intact.

Dr. Richard Williams explains the crucial elements of healthy relationships in his Trust Model:

Many people use the word *trust* to describe a feeling they have regarding interpersonal relationships. Trust does not magically appear in a relationship without certain elements preceding it over time. And once trust has been breached, it is difficult and sometimes impossible to reconstruct.

Three steps pave the path before enduring trust begins. The first step is effective communication. When we communicate effectively, we have an opportunity to move to the second step, which is real understanding. That is when two people have communicated to the point of honest understanding. This can lead to the third step of mutual respect. A respecting relationship demands that each person contribute enough respect that it can be reciprocated back from the other person. Unilateral respect in relationships is temporary and superficial. Mutual respect that can lead to trust is much deeper and must come from understanding. Once a relationship has experienced mutual respect, it is possible for the participants to experience enduring trust. This is a feeling that binds people together over time and through trials.

Integrity	Integrity	Integrity	Integrity
Communication ▶	Understanding ▶	Respect =	Trust

The four steps are contingent or dependent upon the actions or integrity of the individuals involved. If, for example, a person communicates deceitfully, how much understanding will there be? And how much respect will the other person have? Ultimately trust will be lacking.

Enduring trust is a process that takes time and effort. It is clearly the essence of what fuels meaningful relationships. (Richard L. Williams, personal communication with Fay Klinger.)

Forgive the Other Person

Another aspect of being accountable for oneself, and a critical factor in moving forward, is emotionally allowing yourself to forgive your betrayer. Now, at this point you might say, "What? Forgive my betrayer? How can I? He or she ruined my life!"

Ruined your life? No. No one has ruined your life. No one other than yourself has that much power, that much control. Like Grace, the embittered neighbor Barbara told us about in Chapter 4, *you* make the difference. The truth is, you are painfully hurt, but all is not lost. You *can* survive this tragedy, and from here, *you choose* what becomes of your life.

"When Richard left for good, and I realized our relationship was over and that a lot of the burden of raising four children would be on my shoulders," recalls Sarah. "I felt overwhelmed."

But I had enjoyed life before, and now, I didn't want my children remembering their mother as someone always in pain and suffering.

I kept reminding myself that while Richard got me with all of his deception, he did not get *all* of me. No one would ever get all of me. And because of this, I would take the part of me that was still mine and rebuild. In time, I realized that my anger toward him and what he had done was holding me back. I didn't want him to have that much of me either, so I gave that up too. I figured, if God wanted retribution, He could think of ways to punish Richard far better than I could. So I let that anger go into God's hands. If God was not interested in seeking retribution, than I better not be either. That thought helped me let go.

A lot has been written about forgiveness, from the earliest days of the Bible forward, from simple philosophy to commandment—"If ye forgive men their trespasses, your heavenly Father will also forgive you" (Matthew 6:14). More recently, studies have shown the physical and emotional healing power of making peace. Giving up the anger and resentment that comes with holding a grudge can reduce back pain, limit relapses among those battling substance abuse, and slash one's stress level by up to 50 percent. Studies have also led researchers to conclude that harboring bitterness and anger can actually be toxic, whereas letting go can improve a person's energy, mood, sleep quality, and overall physical vitality. Just thinking about forgiving your betrayer may lower your heart rate and blood pressure! (Lisa Collier Cool, "The Power of Forgiving," *Reader's Digest,* May 2004, p. 93.)

According to a Gallup poll, 94% of those surveyed said it was important to forgive. Whether through studies, polls, or firsthand experiences, time and time again, forgiveness is shown to be one of the most effective tools to improve life following traumatic events. (Mark Rafenstein, "Forgiveness: A Path to a Better You," *Current Health*, Weekly Reader Corporation, Dec. 1, 2000.)

Let there be no misunderstanding about what forgiveness is and isn't. Forgiveness cannot fix another person's problem. Forgiveness doesn't mean you accept or condone the offense. Nor does it mean you are willing to continue in the role of being abused or victimized. Forgiveness is not about pretending that things are any different than they really are. Forgiveness is not simply forgetting that the betrayal ever occurred. Nor are you admitting you were wrong. Your negative feelings toward the betrayer will not necessarily be replaced by positive feelings. Forgiveness does not mean you have to trust the other person again. The other person is still accountable for his or her actions. Your act of forgiveness does not pardon him or her for wrongful acts. The right to pardon is only God's—He who fully understands what happened and the intentions of the heart.

Forgiving is a choice; it is all about letting go, refusing to summon up the fiery darts of anger and revenge. It is willfully dropping the practice of obsessing over the injury, and consciously choosing to move on, *releasing* the other person in order to create for yourself a new life with new experiences to think about instead of the old ones. When you forgive, you don't necessarily forget how you were wronged, but you allow yourself to stop dwelling on it. You might continue to see the damage, but only as a part of the whole picture that includes the loving times as well.

Forgiving is accepting the other person for who he or she is, whether you choose to preserve the relationship or not. Forgiving the other person is the most incredible gift you can give to yourself—putting resentment and hostility to rest, handing over the hurt and the judgment to God, and moving on with power.

Todd said, "Forgiveness opened the door to me for what was next in my life. I was completely free to choose my course. The failure of my marriage and the sense of rejection were gone. I felt peace and acceptance of where I was, and the choices Jan made."

Barbara put it this way, "Working through the forgiveness process enabled my heart to heal sufficiently to trust others again. The noblest thing we can do for ourselves and those who have wronged us is to forgive them. When we are angry with someone, it gives them power over us. Replacing the anger with pure love and letting go of the hurt gives us the strength we need to end our suffering and to move from tribulation to triumph."

Dr. Jane Greer offers a reminder. "The decision to forgive is not easily made or quickly achieved. Learning to forgive is a gradual process, not an isolated event; it can benefit both the betrayed and the betrayer. You can't simply forget the heartbreak of a betrayal. But when you forgive the person who betrayed you, you free up the emotional and physical energy you need to feel whole once again. At the same time, you motivate your betrayer to change his behavior so that, if you choose to, you can salvage the relationship on your own terms." (Jane Greer, *How Could You Do This to Me?* Main Street Books, New York, 1998, pp. 166-167, used by permission of the publisher.)

Whitney, the woman who decided to stay with her husband following his years of indiscretions, recalls, "Forgiveness has taken a long, long time. But, through the process of repentance on his part, forgiveness became something I needed to do, for him and for me. It takes a while, but when forgiveness happens, life is completely different. It is so freeing! I could no longer be the judge of this event. I had to let it all go. Now I feel so much more love toward other people."

You know the steps of repentance:
- First, recognize the error of your ways.
- Second, forsake wrongful conduct.
- Third, refuse to repeat the offense.
- Fourth, confess and make restitution where possible.

What are the steps of forgiveness? A simple formula might be:
- First, acknowledge your pain and the desire to forgive—to free yourself and the other person.
- Second, get on your knees in fervent prayer and ask for help.

- Third, reconcile with the other person where possible, or turn it over to God.
- Fourth, choose to let go of the pain and feel peace, concentrating on the positives in your life to create a new beginning without the burden of anger toward your betrayer.

Everyone's healing process is different. Forgiving is an individual experience, obviously depending on the type of betrayal. Some people are able to move beyond the hurt and anger quickly; for others it takes years. Some individuals have the luxury of a sincere apology from the betrayer; others never hear the words "I'm sorry."

An apology can be the bucket of water that drowns the raging fire, if it acknowledges the other person's wrongdoing and is followed by a demonstration of better behavior. But betrayers are sometimes unable or unwilling to look squarely at their actions. Or they are paralyzed by their guilt. They may offer false apologies just to regain your support. Don't be too quick to accept an apology, and don't accept an apology for the wrong reasons, like the fear of losing the relationship or simply wanting to give someone the benefit of a doubt. If the other person is sincere, you will see real signs of change. You can forgive regardless.

On the one hand, with no remorse, apology, or restitution, you can forgive by choosing to remove yourself from the betrayer's reach, letting go of the hurt and the feelings of injustice, and simply giving it to the Judge (God) who knows how to handle it properly. On the other hand, with a heartfelt apology, where the other person makes earnest changes and restitution, you can work through the hurt with new understanding. It's a different kind of letting go because it is open and shared between the two of you. The other person's actions show his or her willingness to earn your trust and to take responsibility. Deal with what is, instead of wishing for what might be. Trust yourself, relying on your intuition, your awareness, and your judgment.

A thoughtful mother wrote about a sweet experience she and her husband had with their ten-year-old daughter, which demonstrates the previous key points:

> Some months ago, Katie approached us regarding an ongoing problem she had been having with a schoolmate. She and a couple of her friends had endured quite a bit of mistreatment at the hands of this child, to the point of being bullied. We advised her that it was best that she and the others separate themselves from this kind of treatment—that they need not allow themselves to be abused. She followed our advice, and later reported that things were somewhat improved.
>
> Then one evening, she again sought our counsel about the same matter. She seemed agitated, frustrated, and generally unsettled. It was apparent that she was harboring much ill will toward her troublesome schoolmate. It became the ideal opportunity for a lesson on forgiveness. We listened, discussed, prayed, and reviewed a few scriptures. When we finished, her whole countenance was transformed. Just employing the idea of practicing forgiveness had given her a large measure of peace.
>
> I would like to share a letter with you that she wrote to her friend following our exchange that evening. (I have changed the names of the other girls in the letter.)

Dear Laura,

This letter is about Jane. We have both had hateful feelings about her. We are mad at her, and it hurts us more than it hurts her. We are at home after school moping about Jane, when she's at home having a good time. When we write her name down and rip it up, or do any other bad thing, she doesn't know about it. She's not hurt. My mom told me a quote about forgiving. The quote is "Being unforgiving is like drinking poison and waiting for the other person to die." Also, forgiving is a commandment we must do. I took a paper with Jane's name on it and ripped it into four pieces. After my mother and father told me all about this, I took the pieces of paper and taped them back together. Then I took another piece of paper and wrote down, "I forgive you. Okay?" I stuck the pieces of paper together and hung them up in my room. Tonight I'm going to pray for her and for me. We must do that every night until we feel better. Also, we need to pray, "Please forgive me for having anger." Remember, even though we forgive her, it doesn't mean we have to play with her when she's mean to us. Well, that's all my information.

Your friend, Katie Anne Hoskisson

(Alison Hoskisson, personal communication with Fay Klingler.)

Forgive Yourself

Forgiving your betrayer is one part of the forgiveness package. The other part, and sometimes the more tricky one, is forgiving yourself. That means you extend to yourself the same grace that God extends to you, the same kindness and charity you are willing to offer the betrayer. You *are* worthy of giving yourself a second chance and of other people giving you a second chance, too. Counter any negative self-talk, and apologize to yourself. Acknowledge what you did or didn't do that contributed to the betrayal. Most likely your intent was only to make life smooth, with no contention, to make it *right,* and it backfired on you.

Forgiving yourself is a choice. Harboring guilt won't change anything, except maybe to increase your chances for more unhealthy relationships. As you disable yourself, you settle for less than you deserve. Continued or excessive guilt also stops the learning process. Like anger, guilt is emotionally paralyzing and does not allow you to move forward or grow.

Guilty feelings are a natural part of the healing process, and to a certain extent can be healthy. But avoid the *if-only* statements—"If only I had been nicer," "If only I had seen all of this coming," "If only I had been more firm." Your betrayer did what he or she did regardless of your good or bad choices.

Bad things happen in life. We have to accept that fact and accept that we sometimes contribute to them. Learn from your poor choices, and vow to make better ones in the future.

"No life is sheltered from the storms of mortality," said Barbara, "yet every one of us has born within us the seeds to succeed."

A deep sense of who I really was, independent of the ex-husband who had wronged me, rose to propel me forward. Gratefully, my self-worth was fairly well intact because I had the insight to know I had *been* wronged, not *done* wrong. Thus, I refused to view myself as he perceived me. Never doubt that I did do a painful inventory to own whatever blame was mine. An honest self-assessment of what I needed to improve upon was prayerfully undertaken. Yet, I did not continue to punish myself with the guilt of being human.

While living in the Middle East on certain religious holidays, I watched men walk up and down the streets beating themselves upon bare chests and backs with chains as blood poured from their wounds. *What change of heart happens with this self-inflicted punishment?* I wondered.

Reliving guilt and punishing ourselves over and over for things of the past does not move us forward. Let the past go; let the unfair wounds heal.

Consider writing yourself a letter. Write about what happened, how you feel about it, and what you are going to do to demonstrate better behavior. For example, "Dear Lori, I am sorry you've been put through such an ordeal. I can't blame you for what Ralph did. I know you did your best under those difficult circumstances. I believe you are entitled to my full support and love..."

Do you see how kind this letter is to yourself? Writing such a letter can help you learn to self-dialogue in a more understanding, gentle, and forgiving way. Another possibility is to make a list of the things you would like to forgive yourself of, and then write specific actions you are going to take to demonstrate your willingness to change.

Forgiving yourself may not be easy, and it may not come quickly. But if you seek it with sincerity and work at it, it will come. Then you will be blessed with a comfort and a peace that is otherwise unattainable.

Acknowledge and support yourself even in the baby steps. Develop the habit of choosing your responses to life's experiences. Make yourself a product of your decisions instead of your conditions. Believe in your ability to learn and move forward, and don't measure what you are or where you are going by looking at others or by looking at where you've been.

The fifth step—Accountability

In fairness, hold yourself and others accountable, and free yourself through forgiveness so you can visualize beyond your past and look with hope into the possibilities of the future.

CHAPTER SIX

The Sixth Step—Advancement

*Some men give up their designs when they have
almost reached the goal; while others, on the contrary,
obtain a victory by exerting, at the last moment, more
vigorous efforts than ever before.—Heroditus*

Healing from betrayal is a process, not a
destination. It is not routine or automatic, like waking
up to a turquoise-mauve sunrise and finding everything
as it should be—an expected, on-schedule, bright, new
day. Instead, it is slow, sometimes agonizing. But, with
effort, even a severely broken heart can be mended and
healed through the sweet passage of time.

Staying in the loop of anger and regrets takes you
nowhere. To heal from betrayal you must let go and
move on to other things. Be patient with yourself. You
won't suddenly forgive. You won't suddenly let go. It's
more like the process of a flower in bloom. Over time,
each petal unfolds, and the flower seeks the sun and
reaches out to grow.

As an old Chinese proverb states, "Be not afraid of
growing slowly, be afraid only of standing still." (Sophie
Bevan, *The Gift of Inner Peace,* Ryland Peters & Small,
London, England, 2004, p. 19, used by permission of
the publisher.)

As Barbara, who experienced the pain of her husband's repeated indiscretions, said, "The kindliest shock absorber while recovering from disloyalty is time—time to take in and process what has happened to you. When tragedy strikes, time almost seems suspended to cushion you until you can take action. During this period of my recovery, I took stock of my situation and moved forward with faith to change it even though I often felt like life was in slow motion. *Would this ever end?* I kept asking myself. *Would normalcy ever replace the chaos of the present?* The resounding answer was *yes!*"

This last step to recovery, advancement, is actually the first step toward your new beginnings. It is purposely taking charge of your life and charting a new course to move forward. While experiences ahead may remind you of the hurt, your desire to forgive and to heal drives you beyond the anger, guilt, and pain. Because of the gift of agency granted by God, there is nothing in your past that can hold back your future happiness, nothing, that is, except your personal choices. No matter what life might have been, it remains a process of growth, and you have today to make it what it will be. It's up to you to purge the painful memories, to seek the sun (a new life filled with opportunity), and to reach out and grow. Now is the time to exercise faith in yourself like never before. Your potential is unlimited!

Martha, who struggled with her husband over finances, expressed her feelings about the healing process this way:

> I still have times when I feel sad. It has literally taken me years to unload. I don't think I'm free yet. Choices...I keep thinking about choices. Why do people make rotten choices when it seems good ones are so much easier? I don't know. But I see my children healing more every

year, and I see myself more able to let go of the responsibility of my former husband's actions.

A few years after the divorce was over, I actually found myself grateful for the ordeal I went through. I never before nor ever since have felt so close to God. I relied on Him in every way. I learned so much about the reality of life, choices, and accountability...I actually felt I had an edge on some people just because of my experience, that somehow I knew something they didn't know—that God was completely aware of me and cared about me, and that if I made good choices, He would be with me, direct me, and open the way for me. It was an awesome, beautiful time.

Visualize Your Camp

Close your eyes for a minute and visualize setting up your desired camp. Imagine not just what it looks like, but how it feels. Where is it? Who is with you? How do you spend your time? Is love felt in your camp? Is there laughter and joy?

One woman, many years ago, visualized her camp as a five-acre flower garden. She saw the big picture— her modest California home surrounded by thousands of radiant daffodils, bringing beauty and joy to an obscure mountainside. To realize the picture she painted in her mind, she began to take action, planting one bulb at a time. She started in 1958. Today this area is called the "Daffodil Garden"—50,000 blooming bulbs cascade over the mountainsides in butter yellow, salmon pink, deep orange, and sunlit gold. Each spring, visitors come hundreds of miles to see the wonder of her camp. Overflowing with gratitude, many call it a life-changing experience as they stand in awe of the indescribable, breathtaking beauty. There were no shortcuts; there was no other way to do it. Year after year, planting one small bulb at a time, this woman forever changed her world. (Jaroldeen Asplund Edwards, *The Daffodil Principle,* Deseret Book, Salt Lake City, 2004.)

Imagination is much more powerful than memory. Even though your memories may be sad, your future happiness is limitless. Imagine *your* big picture. What vision do you have for your camp? What can you do to change your world? An anonymous quote states, "There are no shortcuts to any place worth going." Where are you going? What do you need to do now to get where you want to be, to advance?

Like the Daffodil Garden, the picture you paint in your mind won't be realized by accident. But if you harness your energies, take a chance on yourself, and make deliberate, personal choices, you can invent a future much the same as you imagine. First you must formulate a plan. Then mobilize for change.

The process of making a conscious plan to achieve desired goals has been used by successful people in all walks of life—doctors, lawyers, mothers, dancers, real estate agents, and so forth. People use goals to lose weight, to exercise, to think more positive thoughts, and to have a higher quality of life. Goal setting is important because it creates a focus that motivates people to move forward and change.

Thomas Edison once said, "Being busy does not always mean real work. The object of all work is production or accomplishment and to either of these ends there must be forethought, system, planning, intelligence, and honest purpose, as well as perspiration. Seeming to do is not doing." (http://www.quote world.org/ [March 4, 2005].)

Without goals, your life lacks the forward movement (motivation) that makes you feel purposeful, excited, and alive. When a goal is achieved, horizons widen. As a result, you are empowered with increased energy, hope, confidence, and enlarged vision.

Looking at your imagined camp, do you see yourself in a moving picture of time, accomplishing your dreams and your divine purpose? Are you confidently participating in daily activities that reflect charity, service, and integrity? Do you perceive a feeling of inner peace because you are following God's plan for you? By seeking divine guidance, you make the choice to not just drift along in the hope that life will place you on the right path and face you in the right direction.

Control the Outcome

You've heard it said, "Your actions speak louder than your words." Well, it's true. Your standards, integrity, even your willingness to conform to God's will are reflected in how you use your available time. You may say, for instance, that your family is the most important thing in the world to you. But is it? Are your activities focused on that principle? Do you set times and activities with your family as a priority over things?

Everything you do, whether it is a task or just a thought, takes time. You control the outcome of your life by controlling your time. Allow the leverage of setting long-term goals—goals that fulfill your dreams, your imagined camp, and your divine purpose. And then organize your time to pace yourself to the finish, just like running a race, so you'll accomplish your goals with your personal priorities in place. *Work your schedule around what is truly important rather than try to work what is important into your schedule.*

When you set goals and accomplish them, you feel more in control. The objectives, however, must be yours, not wishes your family or friends have expressed for you. When contemplating your goals, consider the following.

■ Be positive

Express goals in a positive way. "I enjoy thinking good thoughts," is better than, "I have stopped thinking bad thoughts."

■ Be clear and concise

Make your objectives specific rather than vague. "I am in better physical shape," is not as clear as, "I have lost ten pounds." Better yet, "By *x date* I will weigh *x* pounds."

■ Prioritize

When writing your goals, arrange them in order of importance.

■ Be realistic

There are few things worse than setting goals so ambitious they cannot be achieved. On the other hand, setting goals too low seems to say that you feel you aren't capable. A goal should make you stretch a little farther than you thought you could, but not make you feel defeated before you begin.

■ Be kind

Show compassion for yourself and the possible difficulties you might experience along the way. Do not be so rigid that you beat yourself up instead of build yourself up. *Be your leading advocate.*

■ Maintain hope

With consistent effort, poor habits can be replaced with healthy ones. The fear of change can be dismissed by small increments of risk. Impatience can be overcome by long-term thinking and planning.

Follow a Plan

Since written goals are realized far more often than those that remain just in thought or in spoken words, picture again your imagined camp and write down three specific things you can do to work toward making that vision a reality.

Perhaps you want to live in a safe place away from the betrayer. Maybe you want a better job so you can provide for your family. Possibly you picture yourself driving a more dependable vehicle. Turn each of those things into an *I want...*statement, such as *"I want a good job to provide for my family."* Your *I want...*statements become the basis of your written goals.

I want

_____

_____

_____

_____

I want

_____

_____

_____

_____

I want

_____

_____

_____

_____

_____

Take your *I want...* statements and reword them as though you have already achieved them, such as "*I have* a good job that provides for my family."

I _____

_____

_____

_____

I _____

_____

_____

_____

I _____

_____

_____

_____

Now you have three goals written. Some of them may be short-term, others long-term. Where possible, date your goals. Using the example above, you might write, "By October 31st, I *will* have a good job that provides for my family." Remember that you're going to word these statements as if you had already achieved the goals.

I _____
_____
_____
_____
_____

I _____
_____
_____
_____
_____

I _____
_____
_____
_____
_____

Next, write specifically what you're going to do to achieve those goals, back-tracking from the date of each goal's completion. Write in as few words as possible so they can be read and reviewed quickly and easily, such as:

By October 31st, I have a good job that provides for my family.

a) Today I reviewed my accomplishments in life and wrote down a description of my family, my hobbies and interests, my work and service experiences, and my educational experiences.

b) By *x date* I have evaluated the resources I already have and what resources I need to find, including a list of individuals who might be in a position to help me achieve my goal.

c) By *x date* I have contacted individuals from my resource list and brainstormed with them to find job ideas and locations that fit my skills, experience, and availability.

d) Each evening I pray for God's influence that I may find appropriate opportunities, choose wisely, and present myself confidently.

Of course the list goes on, but you get the idea...

Remember, goals are not based on what you have or have not done in the past. They are based on what you want to do, what you want to become, and how you want to behave.

Early in his career, comedian and actor Jim Carey set a goal to become famous. He wrote a check to himself for one million dollars. He dated the check with the year he believed he would be in a position to cash it. By the time that particular year arrived, Jim Carey not only achieved his goal to become famous, he also was able to cash the check!

If you find goal setting too awkward or too cerebral, maybe something shorter and more visual will work, like a mission statement. Your mission statement should include your beliefs and values as outlined in Chapter 3. Identify your life's direction and the opportunities you seek to fulfill that direction. It might be as long as several paragraphs or as short as one concise sentence. For example, your mission statement might be something like the following: "As a person who seeks to live life to its fullest, I enjoy making each day the best day of my life by seeking divine guidance, acting with integrity, showing loyalty to family and friends, leading a successful career, staying safe and healthy, and calmly accepting the challenges that come my way."

For a different approach, as the director of your camp, you could prepare a statement for each of the main elements you believe will encompass the ultimate vision of your camp, like mini-statements. Or your mission statement could be captured in a short list, detailing the values that guide your daily decisions. Here's an example of this concept:

1. Belief—Seek guidance from a loving God and honor Him by my individual choices.

2. Integrity—Speak and perform my duties with uncompromising moral character.

3. Loyalty—Place priority on the time I spend with family and close friends.

4. Ethic—Give a fair effort to all my tasks at home, work, and play.

5. Confidence—Be aware of my surroundings and environment, and build strength of mind and body.

6. Courage—Act without fear, using sound judgment to risk growth.

My mission statement:

_____

_____

_____

_____

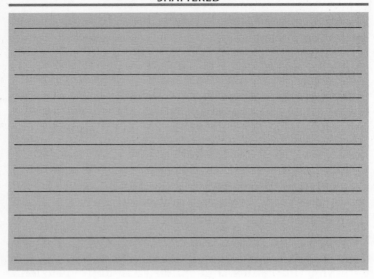

If writing a mission statement is too daunting a task, try jumping forward in your mind to the end of your life, taking a glance back, then envisioning how you would like to be remembered.

Sarah recalls:

When Richard and I were married I had a hard time setting goals. I could never internalize them and make them work. In some ways, they seemed to work against me. But, one time, I heard a woman mention how some tombstones did a good job of defining who the buried people were. For that reason, she wrote her epitaph while young, and used it as a target for living out what she wanted to be remembered for. I could grasp that concept.

Visualizing my life like that seemed appealing to me and so I decided to write one for myself. I thought about it for quite a long time and decided all I wanted my tombstone to say was, "She was a good wife and mother."

Well, this goal became very bothersome to me during and following my divorce, because I felt like, along with all that I had lost, I lost my life's dream. After all, how could I be a good wife if I was no longer married?

Fortunately, a therapist told me that I shouldn't let this goal disintegrate—that my ex-husband making bad choices didn't mean I was a bad wife or that I couldn't be a good wife in the future. He reminded me that I had done my best and acted with integrity, even during the divorce process. He suggested I put the goal on hold, but not destroy it.

Now, after remarrying, even though I am the product of divorce, my life goal to be a good wife and mother remains intact.

A similar approach to writing what you want to accomplish in your life is to consider what you would like to see printed in your obituary.

Once you've written your goals, mission statement, epitaph, or obituary, put them in a place where you can review them often, at least once a day. Rewrite them, if necessary, to clarify them and make them a way of thinking, believing, and acting. You can use your calendar book, palm pilot, or other preferred method for scheduling checkpoints to achieve your goals. At least once a week, as you review your goals, consciously look at your behavior to see if it matches your objectives. When you evaluate how your goals and your behavior match up, recognize the progress you've made instead of the distance still ahead. You can relax and move confidently forward if you plan and follow that plan.

Sometimes the route you choose to accomplish a goal doesn't move you forward. And what may be important to you today may not be significant tomorrow.

As you grow, be flexible. Reevaluate what you want and how you want to get it. Write it down and act on it. If it works, do it some more. If it doesn't work, determine where you are now, what went wrong, and why. Pat yourself on the back for trying. Begin to feel a sense of satisfaction not just for those workable parts that go well and are achieved, but for the times you tried, even if it didn't work. The trying itself is an accomplishment. Look for other options to reach the desired outcome. Allow yourself to risk dreaming, planning, and stretching yourself out of your comfort zone to become what you want. Give yourself the liberty to develop your personal power. If you have established realistic, attainable goals, over time, with a consistent effort, you will realize most of them.

Commit Time and Effort

Most people begin a project like this with enthusiasm, belief, and energy—but seeing their goals to completion is another matter. Too often the vision of what they can accomplish dissipates as their time and abilities are challenged. Remember to believe in yourself. Put the past behind you and start each day with a clean slate of expectations for yourself. Dwell on your positive qualities and use them to your best advantage. Use your strengths to help achieve your goals. Decide to be happy and hopeful. Replace your frustration and worry with action planning. Face life with joy, interpreting opportunities and experiences with a positive sense. Most of your limits are self-imposed and don't reflect your real ability or capacity. Reject the fear of failure and have the courage to act on your individual purpose.

It's not going to be easy. Keep that fact in mind, but only as a shadow to your vision of success. Years ago, there was an inspiring exhibit at the Museum of

Science and Industry in Chicago that illustrated the value of work and determination—a large incubator containing fertile chicken eggs and a few newly hatched chicks. Observers could watch each chick struggle to work its way out through the eggshell and then flop to the floor in exhaustion. It would lie there wet for some time, expending every ounce of energy it had just to breathe. Gradually it would begin to move and would very slowly dry. In time it stood peeping its delight to be alive and would begin working on another goal—finding something to eat!

If the chick were to give up its fight for freedom from the egg, it would die. Similarly, if you give up your fight to succeed, to grow, and to accomplish your righteous goals, eventually your vision will wither and your will to succeed will die. Expect it to be hard, but maintain a passion to finish.

A noted philosopher once remarked that she longed to accomplish a great and noble task, but that it was her chief duty to accomplish small tasks as if they were great and noble.

Your doing needn't be in great leaps. Just like little chips in the eggshell eventually open the way for the chick, little consistent accomplishments directed toward a given target will allow you to maintain a belief in your ability to succeed in reaching that target. Break your goals into specific, achievable parts—parts that are small enough that you can experience some degree of success frequently. The speed with which you head along your path is not as important as the direction you are going.

A reporter asked a 64-year-old ultra-distance runner how he runs a hundred miles. The runner replied, "I don't run a hundred miles; I run one mile a hundred times." Sometimes it works best to focus on running the mile right in front of you rather than thinking about the whole race ahead. A difficult task becomes more manageable when you direct your energy toward completing that piece of the task that you face at the moment rather than wasting energy by worrying about what's to come.

Simplify the things that don't really matter, and organize yourself so you gain control of your day and pace your path to success. Invest enough consistent, concentrated time to accomplish tasks well. If necessary, utilize tiny pieces of available time.

Focus on your most productive time of day. Do you have more energy and concentration in the morning or at night? Be sensitive to your physical and emotional needs. What type of environment do you work best in—alone or with others, with quiet or with a background of soft music?

If frustration overwhelms you despite your degree of effort, go back to the level where you felt successful. When you temporarily return to a level where something feels easy, you regain enthusiasm.

Create Balance

A feeling of harmony comes from maintaining balance. Diminish your anxiety by purposely incorporating into your day activities that help calm you down. It doesn't matter whether you're a business executive, involved in an entrepreneurial endeavor at home, or a full-time, stay-at-home parent. Whatever your position, allow time for pleasure, time to think, time to relax, and time to release the healing powers of your body. Even a short diversion, whether it is spontaneous or calculated, can ease tension and pressure, relax your body systems, and recharge and enlighten your mind. There is a definite relationship between good health and such personality traits as moderation, cheerfulness, contentment, interest in others, and interest in the future. But what may be a happy distraction for one person may be a disturbing annoyance to another. You might think watching television is a waste of time. But your friend may be exhilarated by viewing his favorite programs. You are the only one who can decide when you are wasting time versus when you are relaxing or having fun.

Studies show that creativity is an outlet for relieving pressure and creating inner peace. Consider writing a poem, drawing a picture, designing a flower garden, or building something. Some individuals actually find it soothing to clean house! You might relax by reading a book, watching an inspirational movie, taking a walk, or listening to music.

If you think you're too busy, use caution. Is your *busy* simply an excuse to not have to feel—to not deal with the reality of your life? Slacken your pace to take time to reflect on and appreciate the magnificence of God and His creations, to notice the everyday, rejuvenating joys that surround you. What are you exchanging for your twenty-four hours?

One recovering woman realized what she was missing early one morning:

> As I walked down my narrow driveway, I happened to notice the lawn. It was covered with tiny droplets of dew. Each separate drop of moisture was a little, clear ball delicately balancing at the tip of a blade of grass. I stooped down to marvel at the exquisite sight, then hurried back to the house. My youngest son was the only other person up at that time. I asked him to come outside with me. He quickly put on his shoes and joined me in the front yard. Together we spontaneously smiled and enjoyed looking and talking about one of the marvels of nature. Later, when I returned home from an

errand, the dew had vanished. I realized I hadn't noticed those beautiful, individual balls like that before, yet they had been there at my feet often.

Do you take the time to stop outside to hear the red cardinal chirping to its mate? Or do you reach your hand beyond the eaves to feel the gentleness of an early summer rain? Have you walked outside at dawn and paused long enough to look at the colors of the sky?

Slow your momentum sufficiently to see the beauty around you and to enjoy the companionship of peace.

Part of maintaining balance in your life is taking time to build and bond relationships with family and friends. Slow down your *busyness* to have time to listen, praise, forgive, and love. Is your daily race so swift you haven't time or energy to reach out and give or receive a hug? You know, you can't give a hug without receiving one! Some say four hugs a day for each member of the family will take friction out of the home.

Remember, people and feelings are significantly more important than things done. Realize you are a free agent and responsible for your role in what happens in your life. Remember who and what you are. Believe in the power and the magic within you. Dream of what you are capable of becoming. And work to make that dream a reality by being self-determined, not self-destructive. Seek for balance in your life to diminish strain, to be a more effective, positive you, and to create happiness.

Purposely prioritize your time to develop a working relationship with God through prayer, personal study, and church attendance. With these things in order, you will find peace.

Believe in Yourself

Your mind and body work in concert to make the whole. To be efficient and productive, you must be spiritually, emotionally, and physically well nourished, as well as physically rested. How you maintain your body has a tremendous bearing on your ability to fulfill your goals.

Much of what you do or don't do depends on your ability to visualize yourself accomplishing it and on your attitude. You have tremendous reserves. You are capable of much more than you imagine. As you build physical strength through consistent maintenance, your mental power to visualize your greater abilities will bloom. Your coping power and endurance in all matters will increase.

Whitney recalls her feelings following her husband's betrayal:

> I had to create a vision for myself of who I wanted to be. That changed how I looked at everything around me. Through the betrayal, everything inside and outside of me became so negative that I began to hate myself. But, through the process of time, I could see how destructive this kind of thinking was. My husband had asked for my forgiveness and did abandon all of the things that were so hurtful to him, me, and our family. Eventually, I forced myself to begin looking at the good in me. In doing this, I began to see more and more good in my husband, my kids, and in everyone around me. Once I did this, the good ball kept getting bigger. I even looked with a different eye at all of those people who had offended me, because I felt better about myself. I realized that I have faults, and my hope is that others will forgive me of those weaknesses. Because of this, I decided I needed to forgive those around me. And now, because of this new way of

thinking, everything is going better and I like the new me that came as a result of so much work to overcome so much pain.

Belief in yourself cannot be overemphasized— belief in your ability to learn and advance. It is important to know you can maintain loving relationships and that you can have personal control or power in your life. Hope, belief, and faith are powerful enough to release hormones in the brain called endorphins. Endorphins magnify your energy, drive, and alertness and increase your positive vision of life.

Your attitudes are unconscious habits. If you want to change your life, look at your attitudes about yourself, about others, or about situations that may be holding you back, and consciously decide to change those attitudes.

Most habits are good. For example, habits allow you to do several things at the same time. But when you drastically change your life, old habits that worked in your previous environment may not work in your new environment or with your new experiences. And some habits may lead you away from doing the right thing. Never turn away from what you believe in your mind and heart to be right. And lean on the arm of God to help you make necessary changes as you cultivate new habits and new attitudes.

Lighten Your Load

To ease your burdens, don't be afraid or embarrassed to ask for help. Where appropriate, delegate some of your responsibilities to others. Here's a little activity to help you determine what you can ask others to help you with, and what you may need to do yourself.

To sort out your responsibilities, make a list of all the things you feel are weighing you down. Tear the list into strips so that each separate item is written on its own strip of paper. Now scoop up all the strips in your hands and imagine each strip is wrapped around a heavy rock. Do you feel the weight you're carrying? These are the things you worry about, that weigh you down, that keep you from feeling joy.

Now set down your imaginary stack of paper-covered rocks. One by one, pick up the strips of paper. Read and analyze them to determine if someone can help you with that burden, or if it's even your responsibility to carry at all. The objective is to own what is actually yours, to give away what really belongs to others, and to allow others to carry their share where team effort is appropriate.

As you analyze each item you've written, take three more sheets of paper, each of a different color. Let's say, for the sake of illustration, that you have a green sheet of paper, a yellow one, and a red one. On the green sheet, rewrite those items that you've determined are your responsibility to own and carry. On the yellow one, rewrite those items you can cautiously, tactfully give away or delegate to others. And on the last sheet of paper, rewrite all the responsibilities that rightfully belong to others—those you can get rid of entirely.

Now, prioritize the items you must continue to carry—those items you've written on your green paper. Which ones can or should you do something about today? Make a mental plan of what piece you can do and when. Determine who can help you with the items listed on the yellow paper, and discard any feeling of responsibility for those shown on the red paper. Have you lightened your load?

Serve Others

If you continue to find yourself weighed down, feeling taken for granted, not progressing, or lonely, don't curse the darkness. Get up and be the one to light a candle! Look around you and find someone that is in a worse plight than yourself. Go to him or her and find out what the trouble is. Then, with the wisdom God gives you, try to help that person. And the first thing you know, your gloom will be gone.

Doing something for someone, whether it be community service, such as helping in a soup kitchen or a homeless shelter, or service given to a close friend or family member, like taking the time to listen while he or she vents frustrations, can supply you with genuine satisfaction and joy. One individual said that whenever she complained to her friend about being depressed, her friend would remark, "You need to take a dinner to someone!"

"A source of healing in my life was service at church," said Todd. "Serving others became one of the greatest blessings of my life. It gave me reason for climbing back to happiness; it gave me confidence to know that I was good for something (a message easily drowned out in swimming through the dangerous rapids of divorce). I found that I could bring value to someone else."

You can't help others without receiving something in return—a hug from a happy child, a smile from an ailing friend, a feeling of self-respect, knowing you have made life a little easier for someone else. Again, however, balance is the key. Don't help others to avoid dealing with your own pain and healing. But supplementing your efforts to improve yourself with service to others can help you see beyond your own situation to a clearer perspective.

A lot of simple acts are actually ways of serving others. You can respond to irritation with a smile instead of a frown. You can give warm praise instead of turning away in indifference. You can be patient and understanding instead of quick and abrupt. You can choose to hold back instead of quip in rudeness, stopping the emotional chain reaction of ugly words. You can serve by enduring well. Your steadiness may help others to hold on a little longer instead of giving up.

Saint Francis of Assisi explained the benefits of service in his "Prayer of St. Francis." "O Divine Master, grant that I may not so much seek to be consoled as to console; to be understood as to understand; to be loved as to love. *For it is in giving that we receive*; it is in pardoning that we are pardoned..."

Gradually, as you heal, you will experience more than just survival. You will laugh and enjoy life again. You will advance in faith, find it easier to recognize the needs of others, and develop a desire to reach out and help.

"Once I felt safer and stronger," said Kami, "I started to open up and talk about the abuse."

I know firsthand that women feel very alone at times. So in my healing process, I enlisted a goal to help others. I was on a radio show where I spoke to women in abusive relationships. I told them signs to look for, resources to seek for help, what to expect once they break the tie and leave, where to go for help and assistance, what to watch out for with the former spouse who won't accept the situation, etc. No one deserves to be abused or mistreated.

I also set out to make my children feel safe and secure. I worked hard to get my apartment fixed up. We took our time, saved some money, little by little, to furnish it, and make it a *home* for us. I worked two jobs to get enough money to achieve this. And once I did, I left the second job to spend more time with my children. I tried to do more things *together* with them so we could be a loving family again, making happy memories that will remain with us forever instead of bad memories that could haunt us.

I realized I would rather be happy and poor than rich and miserable. I also realized that material things don't make us who we are. It's what we do with our lives and how we live them to their fullest that makes us who we are.

Keep Your Perspective

Handle today what you can do today. Start slowly and pace steadily so you can finish strongly—like the fabled turtle. When you set goals and achieve them, you gain a sense of value and respect for yourself, and you feel more in control of your life. But don't be afraid to experience the richness of the process of accomplishing those goals. Achieving the end goal is simply a by-product of developing a healthy, vibrant, resourceful lifestyle. Achieve your unique vision by reflecting on the past, having the vision of tomorrow, and doing the tasks of today.

In your mind, imagine your camp once again. Perhaps you see and feel a campfire of warm, good thoughts. The waters of gainful employment provide sufficient income for you to meet your needs. Beautiful skies reflect the calmness you have created. The moon of your inner belief system continues to shine peacefully upon you and watches over you wherever you go.

You must work hard to build such a camp, and then to protect it. Watch for signs of intrusion—someone asking more of you than should be expected, lying, not treating you or your feelings with respect, abusing you through words or actions, not acknowledging what is important to you or supporting you in your efforts to be a good person and lead an emotionally healthy life. When you see these signs, protect yourself from emotional intrusion by politely refusing to be a part of anything that seeks to destroy what you have worked so hard to build. Surround yourself with people who enjoy coming to your camp, those who support what you have created. From time to time, they may give a few respectful, constructive suggestions on how your camp might be a little stronger here or there. But, for the most part, true loved ones come to share your happiness and to contribute to a camp of safety and refuge. Welcome these people into your life, as a part of your inner circle, and deny access to those who obviously seek to destroy your health and well-being.

You must be persistent, conscientious, adaptable, patient, forgiving, and grateful. Focus on the fun and the challenge, not the fear. Remember to trust yourself. You are loved. You have talents. You are beautiful inside and outside. You are capable. Embrace the love God offers. He wants you to succeed and promises to help you. With Him, you can accomplish all that is necessary and claim your true happiness.

The sixth step—Advancement

With belief in yourself, take charge of your life, and chart a new course to move forward and bloom.

Epilogue and an Invitation From the Authors

Shattered is the fragile egg, betrayed.
Left battered, shocked, confused, and dismayed.
Unlike Humpty after his great fall,
Pieces are gathered at the base of the wall.
Encouraged, patched, stronger now than before,
Once again together you can soar.
(After all, a hard-boiled egg is
tougher and better than a raw egg any day!)

In the last chapter of this book, Martha said, "I still have times I feel sad." All of the characters in *Shattered* still struggle to some degree or another. But isn't life like that? Whether our experiences are humdrum or dramatic, calm or filled with trauma, don't we all strive for peace, security, and a rightness in the world around us?

However, Emily, Martha, Sarah, Todd, Enid, Whitney, Kami, and Barbara met what appeared to be defeat with resiliency. What seemed to be a terrible failure led each of them to great opportunities.

Emily became aware of and acted on her worth as a skilled writer and editor.

Martha, utilizing the six steps, came to marry a

gentle, loving man, who practices integrity and respects her right to full disclosure of the family finances.

Sarah's strong belief system and trust in God saw her through the personal rebuilding process with the confidence to marry again.

Todd realized his dreams of a loyal wife, faithful to their mutual religious beliefs, and enlarged his family.

Enid continued her involvement in politics and her devotion to motherhood.

Whitney dedicated her efforts to the forgiveness process and developed a loving relationship with her husband.

Kami, as a single parent, continued to focus on building happiness and security in her family unit.

Barbara married again and experienced love and devotion from her husband and large blended family.

As authors, it is our hope that these six healing steps from betrayal to recovery provide something solid for you to hold on to while you pull yourself out of the world of confusion brought on by betrayal. Awareness, acceptance, action, authorization, accountability, and advancement can take you to a place more centered in tranquil moments and to a fulfillment of your imagined camp.

We wholeheartedly welcome the opportunity to share our experiences of betrayal recovery and the recovery process with individuals and groups. To ask if we can be available to speak, we invite you to contact us through Fay's website, www.fayklingler.com. We can also be contacted through e-mail at fay@klingler.com or bag727@yahoo.com.

Suggested Reading/ Resource List

The following reading/resource list includes information the authors found most helpful in preparing *Shattered*:

After the Affair: Healing the Pain and Rebuilding Trust When a Partner Has Been Unfaithful by Janis Abrahms Spring, PhD., Perennial Currents, 1997, ISBN 0-06-092817-4.

The Betrayal Bond: Breaking Free of Exploitive Relationships by Patrick J. Carnes, PhD, published by Health Communications, Inc., ISBN 1-55874-526-2. A must read for anyone who truly wants to break free of their betrayer.

Blind Trust, the True Story of Enid Greene and Joe Waldholtz by Lee Benson, Agreka Books, Scottsdale, AZ, 1997, ISBN 1-888106-97-2. A compelling true-life story.

Crucial Conversations, Tools for Talking when Stakes Are High by Kerry Patterson, Joseph Grenny, Ron McMillan, and Al Switzler, McGraw-Hill, 2002, ISBN 0-07-140194-6. Fay Klingler's favorite book regarding communication skills.

Dealing with People You Can't Stand, How to Bring Out the Best in People at Their Worst (2nd Edition) by Dr. Rick Brinkman and Dr. Rick Kirschner, McGraw-Hill, 2002, ISBN 0-07-137944-4.

Discussing Pornography Problems with a Spouse: Confronting and Disclosing Secret Behaviors (2nd Edition) by Rory C. Reid and Dan Gray, Mental Health Publications, Salt Lake City, Utah, 2005. [www.provocc.org] ISBN: 1568610653.

Feeling Good: The New Mood Therapy by David D. Burns, M.D., Quill (an imprint of HarperCollins), 1999, ISBN 0-38-073176-2. An excellent resource for redirecting and shaping your thought processes.

Gridlock, Finding the Courage to Move on in Love, Work, and Life by Dr. Jane Greer, Doubleday, 2000, ISBN 0-385-49473-4.

How Can I Forgive You? The Courage to Forgive, the Freedom Not to by Janis Abrahms Spring, Ph.D., Perennial Currents, 2005, ISBN 0-06-000931-4.

How Could You Do This to Me? Learning to Trust After Betrayal by Dr. Jane Greer, Doubleday, 1996, ISBN 0-385-47785-6. A highly recommended book of deep meaning and resource to victims of betrayal.

How to Spot a Dangerous Man before You Get Involved by Sandra L. Brown, MA, Hunter House, 2005, ISBN 0897934474. For future relationships, this book is a must-read!

Living With Your Husband's Secret Wars by Marsha Means, Baker Book House Co., 1999, ISBN 0-8007-5710-6.

National Coalition Against Domestic Violence main office, PO Box 18749, Denver, CO 80218, telephone 303-839-1852, www.ncadv.org.

National Domestic Violence Hotline 800-799-7233.

Tell Me How I'm Doing by Dr. Richard L. Williams, AMACOM, 2004, ISBN 0-8144-0832-X. Dr. Williams is an internationally recognized business consultant, specializing in leadership development, performance coaching, quality and process improvement, and organizational development/diagnostics. He has conducted over 6,000 workshops to more than 250,000 managers and executives around the world. Dr. Williams can be reached at vleadership@earthlink.net.

About the Authors

Fay A. Klingler studied at Brigham Young University and is an author and illustrator. She worked from 1993 to 1995 as a technical writer/editor and project leader for Shipley & Associates (a division of Franklin Quest Co.). Now, while pursuing her creative writing interests, she also works as a bookkeeper.

Fay's previous books include *Daughters of God, You Have What It Takes!; The LDS Grandparents' Idea Book; My Magnificent Mountain; The Complete Guide to Woman's Time; Our New Baby;* and *A Mother's Journal.*

She and her husband, Larry N. Klingler, have twelve children and twenty-four grandchildren in their blended family. They reside in Sandy, Utah.

Bettyanne Bruin is the executive director of the National Coalition for Emotional Abuse Awareness and has written countless local, national, and international newspaper and magazine articles. In addition to *Shattered,* Bettyanne is the author of four books, including *Condolences and Eulogies* and the *LDS Teenager's Guide: 365 Awesome Answers for Today's Challenges.* Bettyanne, along with her husband, Kent, and three of her seven children, live in Sandy, Utah. She enjoys working hard, playing often, and relaxing in all of the many fun atmospheres life keeps providing her.

INDEX

Easy Order Form
CHECK YOUR LEADING BOOKSTORE
OR ORDER HERE

Item	Quantity	Price

Please include $1 shipping for each order.
Colorado residents add 7% sales tax.

___ My check or money order for $_____ is enclosed.
___ Please charge my credit card.

Name _____

Organization _____

Address _____

City/State/Zip _____

Phone _____ E-mail _____

___ MasterCard ___ Visa ___ Discover

Card # _____

Exp. Date _____

Signature _____

Please make your check payable and return to:

Mapletree Publishing Company

6233 Harvard Lane,

Highlands Ranch, CO 80130

Call your credit card order to: 800-537-0414

Fax: 303-791-9028

Secure online ordering:

www.mapletreepublishing.com